MAYFLOWER II

On the Buddhist Voyage to Liberation

by
C.T. Shen

BASIC BUDDHISM SERIES

Published by
The Institute for Advanced Studies of
World Religions
Fort Lee, N.J. and Stony Brook, N.Y.

first edition

These talks have been individually published previously in bilingual English-Chinese editions, by Torch of Wisdom Publishing House, Taipei, Taiwan, R.O.C.

ISBN: 0-915078-03-1

Library of Congress Catalog 83-081198

BASIC BUDDHISM SERIES

Published by
The Institute for Advanced Studies of World Religions

2150 Center Avenue
Fort Lee, N.J. 07024

Melville Memorial Library
State University of New York
at Stony Brook
Stony Brook, N.Y. 11794

Thanks and dedication to

All sentient beings	without them this book need never be published
My parents	without them I could not be here
Buddha Shakyamuni	without him I would never appreciate the truth
Teachers and good friends	without them I would never learn the Buddha's teaching.

I also wish to thank my wife, children, Fayen Koo, Janet Gyatso, and others for their help in making this publication possible.

CONTENTS

PREFACE

This little book presents the experiences and interpretations of some of the important teachings of the Buddha by a person who is an engineer by education, a businessman by profession, and a Buddhist practitioner by devotion, who has a wife, four children, and five grandchildren at the time this preface is being written. In short, he is a common person.

This book is a collection of his speeches delivered at various places in the United States over a period of more than ten years. Some of these talks were published previously under the title *Mayflower;* this new edition includes additional talks and essays, some not published previously. Because the main theme has remained the same, this second collection has been entitled simply *Mayflower II*, and the introduction on the metaphor of the Mayflower journey has been left intact.

The purpose of all of these speeches was to offer to the American public a general introduction to the teaching of the Buddha. Buddha Shakyamuni was a human being who lived more than 2,500 years ago in India, and who solved the mystery of human life. He founded a religion that came to be called Buddhism.

Although this religion was founded so long ago, it appears that its basic teaching may still be accurate and relevant to us today. For example, based on the profound experiences of years of meditation, Buddhist teachers developed a vast system of psychology with more technical terms for the various aspects of mind than are found in most Western languages. Again, the Buddha's teaching of Interdependent Origination is an early predecessor to Einstein's

Theory of Relativity. Most important, however, is the Buddhist emphasis on developing wisdom about the true nature of life and compassion for all living beings, traits that are no doubt much needed in our modern world.

It is sincerely hoped that with this general introduction the reader may find the Buddha's teaching to be just the type of advice needed in the search for a better life and peaceful mind. It might provide a starting point for personal growth and further investigation.

It should be noted, however, that the teaching of the Buddha, and even more obviously the introductory material contained in this book, can serve only as a road map does for an automobile driver. One has to study the map, digest the information therein, and, above all, start the engine and go. One will never reach the destination if one just looks at the map, enjoys its fine printing, but never determines the direction that leads to the destination; or after finding out which direction to go, never lets the car start moving.

The reader is therefore encouraged to contemplate what has been read. Contemplate it with a concentrated mind. If you find a statement that shocks you or makes you laugh because it is exactly what you've been thinking and pondering on, you're probably on the verge of understanding something that can affect you profoundly. Only when what you read or learn becomes a part of your life and way of thinking can you begin to drive your "automobile."

Buddha is a teacher. He uses his finger to point out the moon to us. But if one just looks at Buddha's finger one cannot see the moon. The finger serves simply to point us in the right direction. Once one follows that direction and sees the moon, the finger should be forgotten.

For the same reason, this little book should be given to someone else after you have read it. If you find it useful, let others also make use of it.

Thank you.

C. T. Shen
Fort Lee, 1982

THE MAYFLOWER

Delivered at the Cathedral of the Pines
West Rindge, New Hampshire
July 4, 1976

Dear friends:

On May 14th, the National Day of Prayer this year, I was invited to offer a prayer in New York City. The presentation consisted of three parts: an introduction and background to the prayer; the prayer itself; and the conclusion in which I introduced a verse taught by the Buddha. After the meeting, a young woman asked me why I had chosen that particular verse by Buddha as my conclusion. I responded briefly, but I did not have time to offer her a full explanation. Today I wish to do so.

Let me first read my prayer to you:

May we Americans, in this Bicentennial year, reaffirm the determination of our ancestors; raise our Mayflower flag to sail across the vast ocean of hatred, discrimination, selfishness; and arrive on the other shore of loving-kindness, compassion, joy, and equanimity.

May we Americans, in this Bicentennial year, reaffirm our determination to extend our love of brotherhood to all people on earth, and may we be guided by the collective wisdom of all world religions to save ourselves from self-destruction.

Today our greatest fear is not of nature. Our greatest fear is of ourselves.

The concluding verse by the Buddha was from the

Diamond Sutra (Vajracchedika Sutra). I wish to read this
verse in Chinese:

一切有爲法
如夢幻泡影
如露亦如電
應作如是觀

The English translation is as follows:

> All the world's phenomena and ideas
> Are unreal, like a dream,
> Like magic, and like a reflected image.
> All the world's phenomena and ideas
> Are impermanent, like a water bubble,
> Like dew and lightning.
> Thus should one observe and understand
> All the world's phenomena and ideas.

To answer the young woman's question about why I
chose this verse, I said: "Because this verse is our Mayflower." She nodded with an expression indicating she wished
to say something more, but then other people spoke and the
opportunity was lost. I sincerely hope that my explanation
today will somehow reach her so that she may have my
response.

Before I explain *why* this verse is our Mayflower, I
would also like to read the introduction to my prayer:

> We human beings can send ourselves to the moon,
> but we still cannot eliminate the horrors of a concen-
> tration camp or the need for prisons.
> We spend billions and billions of dollars to elim-
> inate the diseases that kill us, but we pay little attention
> to routing out the motivations that cause us to kill each
> other.

Each time I think of this, I feel very sad. For thousands
of years we human beings have been unable to liberate ourselves from fear! Why? Because we cannot rid ourselves of
hatred, discrimination, selfishness, and desire. But why can
we not eliminate these evils that almost everyone knows
are destructive? The answer is that we human beings have

such a great desire to *possess*. The desire for possession creates attachment. Basically, attachment is due to the concepts of self and possession as when we say "This is mine." This concept of self is strengthened by the belief that both 'I' and the world are real; not only real but also permanent, although we know that is wishful thinking. Surely we realize that no one can live forever and that no one carries money, power, or beauty with him or her at death.

Therefore, to recognize that all phenomena and ideas of the world are unreal like a dream, and impermanent like lightning, is to cause desire and the concept of ego to diminish. When the ego is subdued, hatred, discrimination, selfishness, and desire are also diminished. The ocean is about to be crossed and the horizon is in sight. Thus, this verse of Buddha is our Mayflower to carry us across the vast ocean of hatred, discrimination, selfishness, and desire.

Now may I ask you a few questions? When in 1620 the English were told that there was a beautiful land on the other shore where people could worship freely, and that a boat named the Mayflower was about to sail, did everyone rush to that boat? The answer is no. Millions were suspicious, and only 102 people sailed on the Mayflower.

My second question is: Did the Mayflower arrive in America immediately after she sailed from Plymouth, England? The answer again is no. The Mayflower sailed on September 5th. Gale winds, waves, and a struggle of life and death on the limitless water took place for sixty-six days and nights before the ship reached the new continent on November 10th.

My last question is: What did our ancestors do when the Mayflower arrived in this new land? Did they remain on the boat? No. Naturally, they left the ship and went ashore.

All three questions and answers equally apply to the Mayflower that I am discussing today.

First, of approximately four billion human beings on earth, only very few know about this verse of Buddha, which I call our Mayflower. And even fewer are actually willing to go aboard the ship and sail.

Second, those who do board the ship should not deceive themselves that this ocean of evil can be crossed quickly. It will take a long time and be a hard struggle.

Third, and to this I particularly wish to call your attention, when one realizes that all phenomena and ideas are impermanent and unreal, and when hatred, discrimination, selfishness, and desire are subdued, instinctive wisdom will automatically reveal loving-kindness, compassion, joy, and equanimity. Loving-kindness is happiness for all, compassion is relieving the sufferings of others, joy is happiness at the accomplishments and good fortunes of others, and equanimity, which results from nonattachment, is the calmness of mind in the face of both favorable and unfavorable conditions.

When these realizations are achieved, the ideas of reality, unreality, permanence, and impermanence become meaningless and should be abandoned, just as our ancestors left the Mayflower when it arrived at the new continent.

This service will soon be over. It is impermanent. Tomorrow your recollection of this occasion will be nothing more than a dream. It is unreal. But I hope my message has boarded you onto your own Mayflower. Please carry this message to your family, your friends, and the whole nation. Let us sincerely hope that in the tricentennial year, your children and your children's children will meet here again in a society where loving-kindness, compassion, joy, and equanimity prevail.

Thank you very much.

THE FIVE EYES

Delivered at the Temple of Enlightenment
Bronx, New York
May 25, 1969,
the occasion of the celebration of the
birthday of Buddha Shakyamuni

Dear friends:

What are the five eyes?

Buddhism classifies the eye into five categories; namely, the physical eye, heavenly eye, wisdom eye, Dharma eye, and the buddha eye. It should be pointed out first that the term 'eye' used here does not refer to the ordinary human eye. The human eye is but one kind of physical eye. As a matter of fact, the human eye is not the best example of this category. An eagle has eyes which can see much farther than can those of a human. An owl has eyes which are much more sensitive to light than our eyes, and can see things in the darkness that we cannot see.

In order to illustrate the limitations of the human eye, I shall use a chart prepared by scientists which is called the electromagnetic spectrum (see page 2). This chart tells us that our naked eye can only see a very narrow strip of the universe, called visible light. We cannot see infrared wave lengths and beyond, nor ultraviolet wave lengths and beyond. This means that before man invented the instruments to assist his naked eye in detecting the universe beyond the visible band, the world that he saw and considered complete,

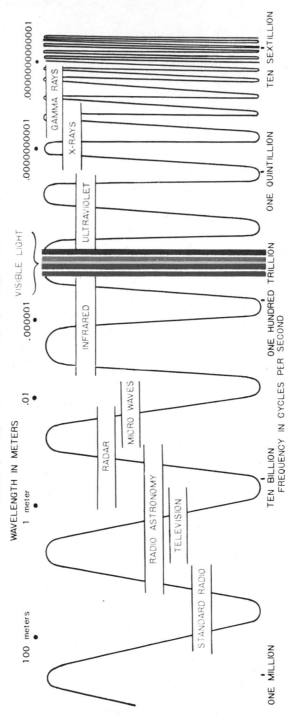

true, and real was actually incomplete and a very small portion of the whole universe. It is really amazing to realize that more than 2,500 years ago Buddha drew this same conclusion without the assistance of any of the instruments we now have.

The following example may illustrate more clearly the inferiority of our human eye, and how it compares with the heavenly eye:

Imagine that there is a totally enclosed dark house in the middle of a big city, with one very small window from which one can see only crowded tall buildings, a little blue sky above, and a few limited human activities. Suppose a child is born and grows up in this house. What would be his impressions of his world? They would no doubt be based on what he sees through the small opening. No matter how eloquently one might describe to him the beauty of the vastness of a seascape and the wonder of a view at sunrise and sunset, he could hardly understand and appreciate them.

This is precisely how our human eye limits us. We are actually in a dark house, viewing the universe through a very small opening which is our physical eye. Yet we insist that what we see is the complete, real, and true world.

Now imagine that there is another house on top of a mountain. The house has a large picture window from which one can see the unlimited sky and infinite horizon. Maybe we can make it even more romantic by saying that numerous flower gardens and dancing girls surround the place. Again, a child is born and grows up in this house. Is it not conceivable that the world he envisions is much greater and more beautiful than the one seen through the small window facing a crowded city? According to this analogy, the second child possesses the heavenly eye whereas the first one has only the physical eye.

Usually it is said that the heavenly eye is possessed by gods or goddesses in heaven. According to Buddhism, however, this statement is not entirely correct because we human beings can also obtain the heavenly eye. There are two ways to achieve it. One way is through 'dhyana,' a Sanskrit word which is commonly (but incompletely) translated as 'meditation.' The other way is to add an instrument to the naked eye (which is also a kind of instrument that can itself be transplanted). Although the first way, meditation, is a much superior method, the second way is probably easier for modern man to understand. Modern man is able to see into remote space by employing a powerful telescope. Modern man can watch the activities of bacteria by using a microscope. Today, one can observe events happening millions of miles away by means of space vehicles and television, and can see many other wonders which in the Buddha's time were exclusive to the heavenly eye. In those days, dhyana was probably the only means of enabling a human being to transcend the boundary set forth by the physical eye. It is clear that Buddha realized that although man's ability to see is infinite, that ability is actually limited by the physical eye. However, through years of meditation, Buddha discovered that the barrier of the physical eye can be broken and that the original ability of man to see can be fully developed. When that occurs, there will be no difficulty in extending one's vision as far as the realm perceived by the heavenly eye.

Up to this point I believe that you can understand the physical eye and the heavenly eye without difficulty. In Buddha's time, it was much more difficult for man to understand the heavenly eye; today, practically speaking, everyone possesses the heavenly eye to some degree. It is, therefore, comprehensible to us.

Now we come to the wisdom eye.

To describe the wisdom eye we need to introduce a very important and fundamental concept in Buddhism, which in Sanskrit is called 'shunyata' and may be translated as 'emptiness.' This is a unique teaching that cannot be found in any other religion.

Voluminous scriptures in Buddhism are devoted to the study of emptiness. What I can offer you today is really a drop of water from a vast ocean, but I will try my best. I will introduce to you three analytical modes of thinking, described by the Buddha on many occasions, which lead to the understanding of emptiness:

1. The analytical method of disintegration.

Allow me to use a radio as an example. Imagine that I have a radio here. If I take out the loud-speaker, can you call the loud-speaker the radio? The answer is no. You call it the loud-speaker. Now take out the transistor. Do you call the transistor the radio? Again no, it is the transistor. How about the condenser, the resister, the plastic case, the wire, etc.? None of these parts are called the radio. Now note carefully. When all the parts are separate, can you tell me where the radio is? There is no radio. Therefore, 'radio' is simply a name given to a group of parts put together temporarily. When one dismantles it, the radio loses its existence. A radio is not a permanent entity. The true nature of the radio is emptiness.

Not only is the radio emptiness; the loud-speaker is too. If I take the magnet out of the loud-speaker, do you call it a loud-speaker? No, you call it a magnet. If I remove the frame, do you call it a loud-speaker? Again no, you call it a frame. When all the parts are taken apart where is the loud-speaker? So, if we dismantle the loud- speaker, it loses its existence. A loud-speaker is not a permanent entity. In reality, a loud-speaker is emptiness.

Now, this analytical method of disintegration can be applied to everything in the world, and will lead to the same conclusion: Everything can disintegrate; therefore, nothing is a permanent entity. So, no matter what name we call a thing, it is, in reality, emptiness.

Buddha applies the method of disintegration to himself. In his imagination he removes his head from his body and asks if the head would be called the human body or self. The answer is no. It is a head. He takes his arm off his body. Would this be called the human body or self? The answer is again no. It is an arm. He takes the heart out and asks whether this is the human body or self. The answer is again no, which we understand now even more precisely since a heart can be removed from one body and transplanted into another without changing one person into another person. Buddha takes every piece of his body apart and finds that none of the parts can be called the human body or self. Finally, after every part is removed, where is the self? Buddha therefore concludes that not only is the physical body emptiness, but the very concept of self is emptiness.

2. The analytical method of integration.

Although we see hundreds of thousands of different things in the world, man is able to integrate them into a few basic elements. For example, based upon chemical characteristics man has classified gold as a basic element. We are able to name thousands of golden articles ranging from a complicated golden statue to a simple gold bar, but all of these articles could be melted and remolded into other forms. They are changeable and impermanent. The things which remain unchanged are the common chemical characteristics, due to which we call all of these articles 'gold.' In other words, all of these articles are integrated under the category of the element which we call gold.

In Buddha's time, Indian philosophers integrated everything into four basic elements, namely, solids, liquids, gas, and heat. Buddha went further and declared that the four elements could be integrated into emptiness. Continuing with our example of gold, Buddha's statement means that we can also question the existence of gold as a permanent entity, even though we have recognized it as a common characteristic of the various golden articles. Whatever we can show is but a specific form of gold, such as a gold bar which is basically changeable and impermanent. Therefore, gold is simply a name given to certain characteristics. Gold itself is emptiness.

By the same reasoning, the Buddha concluded that all solids are emptiness. Not only are solids emptiness, but liquids are too, since the characteristics of fluidity are formless, ungraspable, and empty of independent existence. Thus, 2,500 years ago, Buddha concluded that everything in the universe can be integrated into emptiness.

It is certainly interesting to note that Western scientists have reached a similar conclusion. Before Albert Einstein discovered the theory of relativity, scientists integrated everything in the universe into two basic elements, namely, matter and energy. Einstein unified these two elements and proved mathematically that matter is a form of energy. By doing so, he concluded that everything in the universe is simply a different form of energy.

But what is the original nature of energy? Although I would not venture to assert that energy is the same as emptiness, I would at least like to say that energy is also formless, ungraspable, and analogous to emptiness.

3. The analytical method of penetration.

Buddha performed this method by means of meditation. Meditation may be difficult for most of us, but fortunately today's scientific technology furnishes us with certain analogies which can give us some comprehension of this method. Let us refer back to the electromagnetic spectrum. We know that our naked eye can see only the small portion of the universe which is visible to us, but with the aid of certain instruments, such as an infrared device, x-ray, microscope, etc., modern man is able to see other realms of the universe. To help you understand this more thoroughly, I introduce another chart (p. 10). Here we see an ordinary man as he would be detected by different instruments at different wave lengths. The chart is divided into five sections. Under number one you see an image mainly consisting of red, yellow, and green colors, which is a man as detected by an infrared device. Under two is a man seen by our naked eye. Under three is a man seen through an x-ray apparatus, whereby the skin and flesh disappear but the structure of bone remains. Next to it, marked four, is a picture of the molecular structure of a human body seen microscopically. To the extreme right is an empty space marked five.

Please don't be misled by this chart to think that these various images and the empty space are different entities. They are all the same man. Also don't be misled into the notion that the images occupy different spaces, from left to right. Actually they are all in the same place. To make it more clear, please suppose that I am the man depicted on the chart. Now just imagine that your eyes are able to detect infrared. What you see standing in front of you is a red, yellow, and green colored image. Now shift back to the in-

strument you use daily; my external form is perceived by
your naked eyes. Next imagine that your eyes can see with
an x-ray. My skin, flesh, and blood disappear and what you
see now is the bone structure of my body. Changing to another instrument, the microscopic eye, the man standing in
front of you is a complicated chain structure of molecules.
Now penetrate a bit further. Modern science teaches us that
molecules consist of atoms, and atoms consist of particles,
and ultimately all mass can be converted into energy, the
original nature of which is something that we cannot see
or hold. Let's call it formless form, which is represented by
the empty space numbered five on the chart.

Your attention is invited to the fact that I am the same
man in the ordinary sense, but that I can appear to you in
different forms: colorful image, fleshly body, structure of
bones, assembly of molecules, many other forms correspond-
ing to different realms or instruments, and finally the formless form.

This third method, the analytical method of penetration, again leads to the same conclusion that everything in
the universe can be penetrated to its foundation, called energy by scientists, and emptiness by Buddha.

Now please note a very important point: My discussion so far has been strictly intellectual. However, emptiness is a state of direct experience. It is said that when one
reaches that state there is an experience of tremendous bliss
which is hundreds of times stronger than any kind of bliss
ever experienced by ordinary man. Furthermore, emptiness
is a state in which one transcends the sense of change and
impermanence.

Now let me go a step further. As you may know, the
realization of human suffering was the direct cause which
led the Buddha-to-be, Prince Siddhartha, to renounce his
palace and to become an ascetic in search of the way leading
to the emancipation of mankind. Buddha listed eight kinds
of human suffering, called 'duhkha' in Sanskrit, which has
a somewhat more extensive meaning than the word 'suf-

fering.' The eight sufferings are birth, old age, sickness, death, loss of loved ones and pleasant conditions, association with unpleasant persons and conditions, failure to obtain what one wants, and impermanence. I do not have time to explain the eight sufferings to you in detail, but if you carefully analyze them you can conclude that all eight sufferings are related to, or have originated from, the physical body and consciousness that we call self. The physical body and consciousness of the self are the foundations upon which all human sufferings are built.

Now, if the physical body and the consciousness of self are no longer in existence when the state of emptiness is achieved, how can suffering still exist? When one reaches that stage, everything in the universe, including oneself, is seen as emptiness. All human sufferings disappear, and one is said to possess the wisdom eye.

It's like sudden relief from a deadly heavy burden. It's like the unexpected reunion of a mother with her son who had disappeared for years. It's like the discovery of land on the horizon while one is sailing desperately on a stormy sea. These are a few of the descriptions of the great delights that are experienced when the wisdom eye is gained.

Many disciples of Buddha reached this stage. Such people were called arhats. Although they were saints, Buddha issued a stern warning to them: "Don't stop at the wisdom eye." Buddha explained that with the physical or heavenly eye we see the incomplete, changeable, and unreal world as complete, permanent, and real. Thus we become attached to the world, which is why we suffer. This is one extreme. With the wisdom eye we see everything in the universe as impermanent, unreal, and empty, and like to remain in that state of emptiness. This becomes an attachment to emptiness, and is the opposite extreme. Once there is attachment, whether to a substance or to emptiness, the consciousness of self, which is the root of all ignorance and suffering, cannot be completely eliminated. To obtain the Dharma eye is, therefore, the ultimate teaching of Buddha.

What is the Dharma eye? A man is said to have the

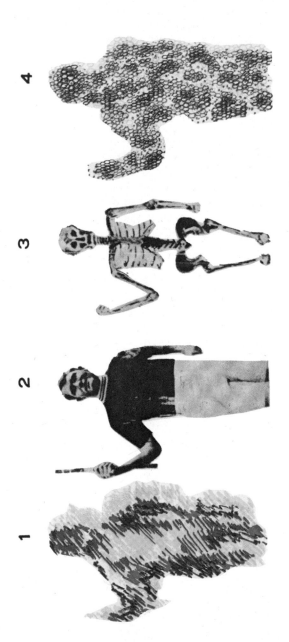

1 2 3 4 5

Dharma eye when he does not stay in emptiness after gaining the wisdom eye. Instead, he recognizes that although whatever he sees in different realms is only a manifestation, it is nevertheless real with respect to its realm.

Let's refer to the chart on p. 10 again. One who has only the physical eye will insist that only the physical body is real, since he lacks the knowledge of all other realms. One who possesses the wisdom eye sees that these forms are phantoms which are impermanent, insubstantial, and unreal, and that emptiness is the only state which is real and permenent. Thus does one become attached to emptiness.

Now, one who possesses the Dharma eye will say that although it is true that all such forms are manifestations, they are not entities separate from emptiness, and they are real with respect to the realm they are in. This realization automatically generates an unconditional, nondiscriminative universal love and compassion. Such a person is said to possess the Dharma eye; in Buddhism that person is called a bodhisattva.

Once one overcomes the attachment to emptiness, the unconditional, nondiscriminating love and compassion arising spontaneously from the direct experience of emptiness is truly a wonder of mankind. This teaching makes Buddhism a most unique and profound practical religion.

Let me tell you a story to illustrate the difference between an arhat who has achieved the wisdom eye and a bodhisattva who possesses the Dharma eye:

A huge mansion is on fire. There is only one door which leads to safety. Many men, women, and children are playing in the mansion but only a few of them are aware of the danger of fire. Those few who are aware of the danger try desperately to find a way out. The way is long and tricky. They finally get out of the mansion through the heavy smoke. Breathing in the fresh open air again, they are so delighted that they just lie on the ground and do not want to do anything more. One of them, however, thinks differently. He remembers that many people are still inside and are not aware of the danger of the fire. He knows that even if they are aware, they do not know the way that leads to safety. So, without considering his own fatigue and risk he goes back into the mansion again and again to lead the other people out of that dangerous place.

This person is a bodhisattva.

There is another famous Buddhist story which has been introduced to Western readers by Professor Huston Smith in his distinguished book, *The Religions of Man.** It goes as follows: Many people are travelling across a desert in search of a treasure at a remote location. They have walked a long distance under the hot sun, and are tired, thirsty, and desperately in need of a shaded place to rest and some water or fruit to quench their burning thirst. Suddenly three of them reach a compound surrounded by walls. One of them climbs to the top of the wall, cries out joyfully, and jumps into the compound. The second traveller follows and also jumps inside. Then the third traveller climbs to the top of the wall where he sees a beautiful garden, shaded by palm trees, with a large pond of spring water. What a temptation! However, while preparing to jump into the compound, he remembers that many other travellers are still wandering in the horrible desert without knowledge of this oasis. He refuses the temptation to jump into the compound, climbs down from the wall, and goes back into the immense, burning desert to lead the other travellers to this resting place.

I believe that everyone here will have no difficulty in understanding that the third person is a bodhisattva.

It should be pointed out here that such compassion is not superficial but is deep and fathomless. It has no prerequisite such as "because I like you" or "because you obey me." It is nondiscriminating and unconditional. Such compassion and love arises from the direct experience of emptiness, the state of perfect harmony, equality, and lack of attachment of any sort.

By this point I hope that you have some understanding of the four kinds of eyes. Here is a story about two famous verses in Zen Buddhism:

*New York: American Library, 1958.

The Fifth Patriarch in the Tang Dynasty of China once asked his disciples to write a verse to present their understanding of Buddhism. The head monk Shen Hsiu presented one as follows:

The body is a wisdom tree,
The mind a standing mirror bright.
At all times diligently wipe it,
and let no dust alight.

The Fifth Patriarch commented that Shen Hsiu had only arrived at the gate and had not entered the hall.

A layman called Hui Neng was also in the monastery. Although he had not yet received instruction from the Fifth Patriarch, he was nevertheless a highly gifted person. When Hui Neng heard the verse, he disagreed with Shen Hsiu and said, "I have one also." He submitted this verse:

Wisdom is no tree,
Nor a standing mirror bright.
Since all is empty,
Where comes the dust to alight?

Later, Hui Neng became the Fifth Patriarch's disciple and achieved enlightenment. He became the famous Sixth Patriarch of Zen Buddhism. He gave different teachings to persons of different capacities. Although there is no such record, I would venture to say that the Sixth Patriarch would have had no hesitation in telling a beginner who requested instruction that

The body is a wisdom tree,
The mind a standing mirror bright.
At all times diligently wipe it,
And let no dust alight.

Now, with what kind of eye did Shen Hsiu present his verse? With what kind of eye did Hui Neng disagree with Shen Hsiu and present his own verse? And why, after he had become Sixth Patriarch would he use the one with which he had disagreed before? What kind of eye was the Sixth Patriarch employing now? I will not answer these questions but would like to leave them with you so that you might find your own answer.

Now we come to the buddha eye.

So far I have managed to say something to you about the four kinds of eyes, but there is really nothing I can say about the buddha eye because whatever I say will miss the point.

But I also know very well that I cannot just stop here, say nothing, and raise a golden flower like Buddha did. Not only do I not have the kind of radiation to convey understanding through silence, but also you will not be satisfied. It is understandable that just as we all have the physical eye, we all have the physical ear and the physical mind. I therefore have to say at least something.

You will notice that in our discussions about the first four kinds of eyes, there was always a subject and an object. For example, with the physical eye we have a human being as subject and worldly phenomena as object. With the heavenly eye we have divine beings as subject and the vast realms of space as object. With the wisdom eye we have arhat as subject and emptiness as object. Bodhisattva is the subject and the various realms of the universe are the objects when we refer to the Dharma eye. When we talk about the buddha eye, however, it would be quite incorrect to say that buddha is the subject and the universe is the object, because the distinction no longer exists between buddha and the universe. Buddha is universe and universe is buddha. It would be equally wrong to say that buddha possesses the buddha eye because there is again no distinction between the buddha eye and buddha. Buddha eye is buddha and buddha is buddha eye. In short, any duality you can construct is not relevant to the buddha eye.

The second point I wish to make about the buddha eye concerns the nature of infinite infinity. What do I mean by infinite infinity? Although we say that the human concept of the cosmos is an infinity, such a concept is just like a bubble in the vast sea when compared with Buddha's experience of the cosmos. Is it incredible? Yes, it is incredible. But let's think of what we have in mathematics. You know that the first degree of power is a line. The second degree of power is a plane. The third degree of power represents a three-dimensional space. All of these shapes could already be infinite in size. Now how about the fourth degree of power, the fifth degree of power, up to the nth degree of power? If you are able to explain what the nth degree of power represents, you might have some understanding of Buddha's cosmology: the infinite infinity.

Thirdly, I wish to say something about the nature of instantaneity and spontaneity. This is again a concept that is very difficult for human beings to understand. To us, the duration of time is a solid fact. Moving through this time factor, man grows up from an infant, to a youth, to maturity, to old age, etc. It is beyond our comprehension to say that time does not exist for the buddha eye, but that is what the buddha eye entails. Billions of years are no different from one second. A world which is measured as billions of light years away from the earth according to our cosmology can be reached in just one instant. What a wonder this is!

The final point I wish to make about the buddha eye is its nature of totality and all-inclusiveness. Some of you might have seen a movie called "Yellow Submarine." A monster which is like a vacuum machine sucks in everything it encounters. After it has sucked in everything in the universe, it begins to suck in the earth on which it stands. The vacuum machine is so powerful that it sucks the whole earth into itself and finally it sucks itself in. This image illustrates the all-inclusiveness of the buddha eye.

Now, let me summarize. I have mentioned four points about the buddha eye:

1. no subject and no object; that is, no duality
2. infinite infinity; that is, no space
3. instantaneity and spontaneity; that is, no time
4. all-inclusiveness and totality; that is, no nothingness.

These are the four essential concepts of the buddha eye, if we must express it in words.

Before I conclude today's talk I would like to tell you another story.

A couple was always at odds with each other. Then

they heard about the five eyes. One day they began to quarrel. It looked as if it would be one of their usual arguments with both husband and wife so upset, angry, and frustrated that they wouldn't speak to each other for days. Suddenly the husband said, "I am using my heavenly eye now. You are just a skeleton. Why should I argue with a skeleton?" The wife kept silent for a while and then burst into laughter. The husband asked, "What are you laughing about?" The wife said, "I am using my wisdom eye and you've disappeared. Now there is nothing bothering me. I am in shunyata." Then they both laughed and said, "Let us both use our Dharma eyes. We are all manifestations, but let's live happily together in this realm."

Today we are celebrating this great man, Buddha Shakyamuni's birthday. Reverend Chi Hoi is going to deliver to you a big birthday cake. I am only giving you some birthday candy. My birthday candy is this advice: Don't always use your physical eye, but broaden your view. Do not let your mind always be carried away by what you see in this narrow band of "visible light." Break this narrow perception. Broaden your view. Develop and open your heavenly eye. Gradually develop and open your wisdom eye. At that point please remember our numerous fellow men and other poor creatures struggling in the immense burning desert of birth and death. Open your Dharma eye! Eventually I hope that all of you will have the buddha eye, and will reach the highest state of enlightenment so that you are capable of leading the numberless sentient beings in infinite space to buddhahood as well.

Thank you.

A GLIMPSE OF BUDDHISM

Delivered in a joint assembly of two Catholic high schools
New York, New York
April 10, 1970

Dear friends:

According to Webster's dictionary, religion is "the service and adoration of God as expressed in forms of worship, in obedience to divine commands, and in the pursuit of a way of life." There can be quite a few definitions of religion, but if the above definition is applied, then Buddhism cannot be classified as a religion because Buddhism does not teach that there is an almighty God who gives commands and whom man should obey.

Buddha is not an almighty God. Buddha was a human being born 2,514 years ago in ancient northern India, today's Nepal. He was a prince who, at the age of twenty-nine, left his palace in search of ways to liberate human beings from suffering. He achieved complete enlightenment when he was thirty-five. For the next forty-five years, until the last minute of his life, he preached to all kinds of people, beggars and kings, without the slightest discrimination. He preached about his discovery—the truth of the universe and the meaning of human life.

Buddha, far from being an almighty God, is an example of what human beings can achieve. The image of Buddha that one sees in a Buddhist temple serves as a memorial and as a reminder that every human being can achieve the same enlightenment that Buddha achieved. So in Buddhism such statues are not actually worshipped, but rather are respected as symbols of enlightenment.

In the *Diamond Sutra*, which is one of the most popular scriptures in China, Buddha made this point clear:

> Whoever identifies me by any visible form,
> Or seeks after me by an audible sound,
> Is walking on a wrong path,
> And will not be able to see the buddha.

What did Buddha discover when he attained enlightenment? To try to answer this question would be to be like the baby tadpole who can only mimic his mother's words. A mother frog leaves her young swimming in the pond and goes to the bank to enjoy the gentle breeze and warm sunshine of the spring day. When she returns to the pond, her babies crowd around her, yearning to learn of her experience in the great beyond. But try as she may to explain the exquisite feelings and sights on land, the young waterbound frogs cannot manage to really understand what her experience has been. They can repeat her words to themselves and others, but they will only know the true meaning when they have developed their own legs and can leap to the bank of the pond themselves. In the same way, Buddha found that human language is inadequate to describe the state of enlightenment. One has to find enlightenment by one's own experience.

However, that does not mean that Buddha said nothing. In fact, his teachings are so enormous and rich that no one has yet been able to summarize and condense them into one book. Today I am trying to introduce to you only a few concepts which I hope will provide you with a foundation for further exploration, if you are interested.

Buddha described to us two very fundamental discoveries. His first discovery is that the world which man recognizes in daily life is only a very small section of the whole universe. It is far from complete. Because of this incompleteness, man obtains a distorted knowledge and is very much misled. The second discovery is that the human

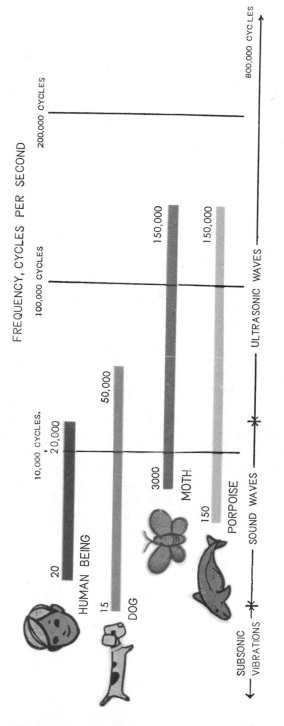

being does possess the ability to discover the complete and undistorted universe and can therefore liberate himself from all kinds of sufferings, including death, which are the results of distorted knowledge.

Before we go further into such a highly philosophical discussion, may I ask you one question? Is there anything in this open space just in front of me? If you were someone who lived a few hundred years ago, you would most likely reply: "No, it is empty. There is nothing in this space." Today, however, most of you will have a different view. Some of you will say there is air in the space. One who has studied chemistry will go a step further by saying that there are present oxygen, nitrogen, and possibly H_2O in vapor form. A young girl of seven or eight years will not surprise you if she says: "I know there are also radio waves because the radio talks when I put it there." A physicist will say much more, referring to atoms, electrons, cosmic rays, and many other scientific names which would puzzle even modern man. Now what does all this mean? It means that this open space is full of things and activities that the naked eye cannot detect. The human eye cannot see the complete universe. It sees a very incomplete world and so the information we are getting is very incomplete.

Let me give you another example. Would you not say that when you look at me, you are seeing a solid physical body? However, your eye is again giving you an incomplete picture. Have you ever thought that this body that stands here is actually a combination of approximately 65% water; more than 10% minerals, mainly calcium, phosphorous, and iron; about 10% gas; plus hydrocarbons and other elements? To use a currently popular term, would it not be more correct to recognize me as a mass of highly polluted water than as a solid body? But your eyes certainly do not give you that impression.

2,500 years ago, Buddha had tremendous difficulty in convincing people that their eyes did not give them a complete view of the universe and that they were misled. Today people are no longer that ignorant. When I delivered a talk

("The Five Eyes") at the Temple of Enlightenment in the Bronx, New York last year, I presented an electromagnetic spectrum chart (see p. 2) and showed that our naked physical eye can only detect the very small portion of the universe that we call visible light. People understood immediately that our vision is terribly limited by our physical eye.

Not only does our eye not perceive a complete picture, but our other sense organs also perform very limited functions. I refer you to my sound reception chart (see p. 19) which gives you the range of sound frequencies detectable by various animals, including human beings, dogs, moths, and porpoises. The frequency of a sound is the number of cycles per second of a sound wave. The higher the frequency, the higher the pitch. The first thing which you probably notice is that a dog can hear much more than can a man. A dog hears sounds of frequencies between 15 and 50,000 cycles per second, but man hears only those between 20 and 20,000. A dog can hear many high-pitched sounds that are silent to man. This is one of the reasons why certain animals have a much better chance of survival in the wild than man does. It is interesting to note that a moth is able to detect very high pitches, up to 150,000 cycles per second, which is 7.5 times the highest pitch man is able to hear. A moth's (or a porpoise's) world of sound must be fantastic by human standards. Thus, I believe that we can all agree that the human ear hears only a very small portion of the universe, just as the human eye sees only a very small part of it.

The three other senses of the human being contribute even less information. As a matter of fact, man's sense organs of taste and smell are much inferior to those possessed by most animals. This is why Buddha said that the world man recognizes in daily life is only a very small section of the whole universe and is far from complete. Man's information is most likely distorted and he can be fatally misled.

Someone might ask what is so harmful about incomplete knowledge. Some will say that a few hundred years ago men did not have the kind of knowledge about the universe that we have today, yet they survived nevertheless and most probably lived a happier life than we. This statement could well be true, but before we decide that it is, let us consider this story.

There is a famous tale in India called "The Blind Men and the Elephant." I am sure many of you know it already. A king summoned a number of blind men who had no idea of what an elephant was. The king asked them to stand in circle around an elephant, each man touching a different part of the animal. Then the king said: "This is called an elephant. Now tell me what an elephant is like." The blind man who touched the side of the elephant said that an elephant was like a wall. The one who grasped the long trunk was frightened and said with a trembling voice: "Oh no, it's like a giant snake." The blind man who examined the tail with his fingers said: "Not exactly. I would say an elephant is like a small snake or rather a rope." Then the shortest man who was only able to hold the leg of the elephant, said: "My king, an elephant is just like the trunk of a tree."

Now may I invite your attention to a very important point: If each of the blind men realized the fact that what each touched was only a part, and not the whole elephant, and that the part each examined resembled something else, then all that the blind men said would be correct. What made them wrong was that each thought he was examining the whole elephant. Thus the findings of each become wrong, his statements incorrect, and his emotional reactions, such as fear of a giant snake, inappropriate.

The incomplete and distorted information perceived by our sense organs can be very dangerous. I can give you many examples, but will mention just a few. Man cannot avoid the flu because he cannot see the viruses in front of him, and just goes ahead and assimilates them. Man creates racial problems because of the slight differences in skin color without knowing that we are all basically the same (we all are about 65% water and are highly polluted). Man fights with others because of the conflict of interest between the subject 'I' and the object 'you,' without knowing that the distinction between 'I' and 'you' is a wrong concept which is the result of distorted and incomplete information received by our sense organs and misinterpreted by another organ—the brain.

The point I wish to get across to you is that unless we recognize the fact that we are fooled by our sense organs and by our chief of staff, the brain, we have no chance of changing the course of our lives and liberating ourselves from all human suffering, including the cycle of birth and death. As soon as one recognizes this fact, a single question naturally comes to one's mind. How can man discover the complete universe?

Buddha, based upon his own personal experience, provided an answer to this question. This answer is the second fundamental discovery of Buddha which I said I would introduce to you. It was realized by Buddha when he reached supreme enlightenment. Records show that Buddha discovered that every man has the same basic ability (which in Buddhism is called 'buddha-nature') and is endowed with the capacity to know the complete and infinite universe just as Buddha experienced it. Only man's ignorance and tenacious attachment to wrong views resulting from incomplete and distorted information prevent his basic ability (buddha-nature) from unfolding fully. However, at enlightenment, ignorance and tenacious attachment to wrong views disappear, enabling man to discover the complete universe.

You might like to ask: What is buddha-nature? Buddha-nature is precisely the very state of enlightenment which cannot be described or discussed but can only be realized by one's own experience. We know from Buddha's teaching that every human being, in fact every sentient being, possesses the same buddha-nature. Therefore, all sentient beings are the same. Now this point is extremely vital. Because of this fundamental understanding, Buddha taught that we must not kill. Because of this fundamental understanding, Buddha's teaching provides a foundation of optimism, courage, compassion, and love for mankind.

Although buddha-nature is indescribable, Buddha's teaching indicates at least two of its basic characteristics. One is freedom from attachment, and the other is freedom from limitation. Today I will only be able to give you some idea about freedom from limitation. I will say a few words about freedom from limitation in space and freedom from limitation in time.

1. Man's basic ability has no limitation in space.

Let us examine, for example, man's ability to hear. One of the farthest sounds man's naked physical ear can possibly hear is thunder originating in a remote cloud. It could be several miles away. A few hundred years ago no one would doubt the statement that man's ability to hear is limited to a distance of several miles. Today our belief is entirely different. We know from biology that there is no essential difference between the human ear and a mechanical or electrical device. So when the telephone was invented, the distance from which a sound could be heard was greatly increased by replacing, so to speak, the physical ear with a combination of ear and telephone. When the first Americans set foot on the surface of the moon, this distance was extended to about a quarter of a million miles by employing certain electric and electronic devices to extend man's physical ear. It is apparent to everyone now that there is no limit as to how far man can hear. It depends upon what kind of instrument he uses. Thus, man's basic ability, i.e., buddha-nature, has no limitation in space.

2. Man's basic ability has no limitation in time.

Man has known for a long time that in dreams we can see and talk with someone who is deceased, but we would say that this communication is a dream and not real life. Today, however, the practice of electrical stimulation of the brain reveals the startling fact that by stimulating certain brain cells with electrical impulses, one not only can see and hear without using one's physical eye or ear, but also can vividly recall events which occurred in the past. Furthermore, the brain cells can be activated in parallel so that a number of events can be revealed at the same time, just as when a number of electric lamps are connected in parallel, all the lamps light up when the circuit is on. Such technology brings man's understanding a step closer to what Buddha described, i.e., that the past, present, and future can be revealed in one instant. The basic ability of human beings, our buddha-nature, has no limitation in time.

Modern science has already contributed a great deal of information to support Buddha's discovery that man's buddha- nature has no limitation and that man does have the ability to detect a much more complete universe than his five unaided sense organs and brain can do. Furthermore, modern science is developing more and more sophisticated theories and devices to enlarge man's contact with, and understanding of, the universe.

At this point I wish to say a few words about modern science upon which I have so heavily relied in explaining Buddha's teaching. Would it be possible that future developments in the field of modern science could bring human beings closer to the state of enlightenment? Could science help us to unfold our buddha-nature or basic ability, a feat which Buddha accomplished through meditation? My answer is both yes and no.

I would say yes because scientific knowledge and technological development help man greatly to understand more about the universe. For example, it is much easier for me to explain Buddha's discoveries today. I would say no because science is still an activity within the boundaries set forth by the physical world which man recognizes. For example, velocity has a limit. Nothing can move faster than 186,000 miles per second, which is the velocity of light or electricity. Another example is absolute zero. No temperature in the universe can be colder than minus 459.7 degrees Fahrenheit. Further, there is another limit which I believe is far more serious than these physical limitations, and that is the fact that scientific activities still work within the sphere dominated by man's brain, which always provides the concept of self. The human being is the center of all scientific activities. Like the theologians who have to work within the concept of God, the scientists have not gotten rid of the ego. Unless it can break through such limiting barriers, science will only be able to help us understand a little of what an enlightened one like Buddha said, but will not be able to bring us to the state of enlightenment. It is my humble opinion that even with today's marvelous scientific accomplishments we still have to go through the practices Buddha taught if we wish to achieve enlightenment. However, the help of scientific knowledge is analogous to that of the steamboat by which man can reach the other shore of the vast ocean more easily than by relying on the sailboat of thousands of years ago.

What kinds of practices did Buddha teach? There are, in fact, very many. One of the fundamental methods taught by Buddha is 'dhyana.' Again there are many variations within this broad category.

The English word 'meditation' is almost an equivalent of dhyana. It refers to the state of pure concentration of mind, and involves the cultivation of keen awareness, vigilance, and intuitive observation. Today I wish to introduce to you a simple meditation method. This method is called "counting the breaths."

We breathe in and out all the time, but we are never mindful of it. When practicing this meditation method, try to count your breathing. When you breathe you sometimes take a deep breath, sometimes not. This does not matter at all. Just breathe in and out as usual without effort or strain. Count only when you breathe in, not when you breathe out. Each inhalation counts as one. When you finish counting to ten, repeat the process starting from one. Try doing this continuously for fifteen minutes every day and gradually extend the time to a longer period as you wish.

Although you may practice this in any posture, such as lying down, I recommend that you sit with your body erect. Don't be stiff or push out your chest. Preferably you should sit crossed-legged, because that is the best posture to achieve physical and mental equilibrium, but this is not a necessity. Put your hands comfortably on your lap, overlapped with thumbs touching each other. You should not lean on a wall or chair back. You may close your eyes, or you may open them slightly and gaze without effort at the tip of your nose.

At the beginning you may find it difficult to count

continuously up to ten. Very often your mind will run away, and you will lose your concentration on counting. Do not worry about it. Count from one again when you regain your awareness of counting.

I can hardly describe the vivid experience you will have one day. For a split second the counting, the breathing, yourself, and the outside world will all vanish. Only pure awareness remains. This moment will be a tremendous experience for you, full of joy and serenity. However, as soon as you regain consciousness of yourself, you will immediately lose the experience. It will take days for you to experience it again. But this kind of experience will be repeated again and again, for longer and longer periods. The clouds will begin to thin and disperse, as the sunshine penetrates here and there. A good foundation is then established, and you are prepared for advanced meditation. Enlightenment may still be far away, but the wind is now with your sail.

I have thus far introduced to you two of the Buddha's discoveries. First, our sense organs and brain present us with an incomplete, distorted, and misinterpreted view of the universe, resulting in human misunderstanding and suffering. Second, a human being does possess the ability to discover the complete, undistorted, and true view of the universe. I have also introduced to you a practical method which one day may lead you to unfold your original ability to realize the universe completely and truly.

All this is fine, you may say to me, but it is so remote from my daily life that it is hard to comprehend. We are living in this environment no matter how incomplete and untrue. How could such highly sophisticated knowledge help us?

Dear friends, you are absolutely right, but I have one remark to make. In my limited experience, I have found many people who have doubts about the reliability of human sense organs and who have had some experience of mystical power. Such people are like travellers at a crossroad who suddenly realize that they have found the right direction to take, even with just a little knowledge such as what I have

given you today. You could be one of those persons. So try
to spend a few minutes each day practicing the counting of
your breaths. It is good for your physical health, relaxation,
sound sleep, tranquility, and efficiency in your daily work.

In addition to meditation, I would like to give you two
further suggestions. These are not the main engine of the
ship, but they could be very important auxiliary engines.
In fact, you are probably practicing them every day, although on a minor scale in comparison to what I am going
to suggest, and you may not be aware that you are doing
so.

The first suggestion is called 'dana' in Sanskrit, which
is usually translated as 'alms' or 'giving,' but has a much
broader meaning. It is very close to the 'great love' taught
by Christ. In Buddhism there are three kinds of giving: 1)
giving of material things to the needy, to free them from
the suffering due to the lack of material things; 2) giving
of knowledge, that is, imparting proper knowledge to others
to free them from suffering due to ignorance; and 3) giving
of fearlessness, that is, helping others free themselves from
fears, of whatever nature.

The key to giving is not—may I repeat—is not to give
to others in expectation of a reward for yourself. For the
enlightened ones, giving is a spontaneous action arising
from compassion and love; and for us ordinary people giving
is self-training aimed at reducing and eliminating our false
concept of self which is the root of human suffering. As
Buddha said, attachments cloud the buddha-nature, and the
concept of self is the worst and most deeply rooted attachment. Egoism is, therefore, the worst hindrance to liberation. Giving is a sharp sword to kill egoism.

It is interesting to note that everyone has a 'Great
Dana' once in his life. When I say Great Dana, I mean that
one has to give up completely everything that one possesses—all power, even if one is the dictator of the most
powerful country in the world; all money, even if one is a
billionaire; all beauty, even if one is the most beautiful
woman in the world; and everything one has, even if one is
the most greedy and stingy of men.

Now what is this Great Dana ? It happens at the time of one's death. Not a single thing, no matter how small or how beloved, can we take with us. Unfortunately, very few of our fellow men realize this fact, and so the Great Dana is usually compulsory and painful. Doesn't it make sense that such compulsion and pain could be greatly reduced if one were accustomed to giving during one's lifetime?

The second suggestion I have to give you is a hint as to how you can free yourselves from bondage of any sort. This hint is better conveyed to you through a story so that you may make your own interpretation. It happened in China about one thousand years ago, and for better understanding I will give you some background information. At the time this story took place, the social relationships between men and women in China were very strict. You may have heard that girls seldom went out of their houses before marriage. This kind of restriction was especially enforced in Buddhist communities. In one of the sects of Buddhism at that time in China the monks were not allowed to laugh or smile at a woman. They could not touch a woman's body or expose their chests or legs in front of a woman. If they did, they would be committing a sin. My story is as follows:

There were two monks of middle age, each of whom had had many years of study and training in a Buddhist monastery belonging to the above-mentioned sect, so they knew those precepts very well. One day they were travelling on foot. It was late afternoon when they arrived at a river. There was no bridge or ferry, but the river was shallow and they believed they would have no difficulty in wading across it. Suddenly they saw a young lady who was attempting to cross the river too, but was hesitating to step into the water. She was in trouble. One of the monks went to her and offered to help by carrying her across the river on his back. The other monk was very much surprised by what his brother monk had done. Puzzled and frustrated, he was very unhappy as he followed them to the other shore of the river. The first monk put down the lady, who thanked him and left. The two monks continued their journey. While walking, the second monk could not forget the incident. He wondered how his brother monk could violate the precepts that they had observed for so many years. What a grave sin he had committed, and even in another's presence! Could it possibly be that he violated other important precepts when he was alone? It was about dark now and they found an abandoned temple. They were tired and went into the temple to lie down. The first monk immediately fell asleep but the second one could not. First he was frustrated, then he felt pity for his brother monk for committing such a grave sin. He tried to pray for him to reduce his sin but he imagined all kinds of things. He tossed fretfully and could not get to sleep. At about dawn, he heard the snore of sound sleep from his brother monk, and he became very angry. He made a noise which woke the first monk. "What happened to you, my brother? Why aren't you sleeping?" The second monk answered angrily: "Do you know what you have done? What are our precepts? How could you hold a girl on your back and wade across the river? I could not sleep because I was trying my best to pray so as to minimize your sin, but you simply don't care and have been sleeping soundly." The first monk replied, "Oh, you are talking about that lady. I dropped her a long time ago as soon as we crossed the river, but why do you, my brother, still carry her on your back?"

Thank you very much.

SOME KNOWLEDGE ABOUT BUDDHISM

Delivered at Christ Church Parish
Ridgewood, New Jersey
November 1, 1978

Dear friends:

You probably all know that China is a nation in Asia. How many of you know the Chinese character for the word China? It is Chung Kuo (中國). Literally, *chung* means middle or center, and *kuo* means country or kingdom. Chung Kuo is, therefore, the Central Kingdom. For thousands of years, the Chinese believed their country to be the center of the world and their emperor, whom they usually referred to as the Son of Heaven, to be the highest authority on earth. So it was that the Chinese believed that all people inhabiting areas other than the central kingdom were inferior and that their rulers were subordinate to the emperor of China. If, during that period, someone had proclaimed that there were many emperors on earth, some even more powerful than the Son of Heaven, his head very likely would have been chopped off.

It was not until the beginning of the eighteenth century, when Western civilization reached China, that the Chinese began to realize that there were many nations on earth with many powerful rulers. The Chinese were no longer in an "ivory tower"; their perspective was broadened; they shared with other nations the responsibilities of the world. It is, however, important to note that regardless of that recognition, the importance of their own head of government was in no way diminished in the minds of the Chinese. To this day, their own leader is still the most important and influential person in their lives.

On another note, just a few hundred years ago everyone thought that the sun was the center of the universe. Today, however, astronomers tell us that the solar system as we know it, with the sun, the earth, and her sister planets, is merely a small group of celestial bodies at the edge of a galaxy called the Milky Way, which consists of more than 100,000 million stars like the sun. Furthermore, the Milky Way is only one modest member out of thousands of millions of galaxies in the universe. So we understand that there are countless suns. It is incorrect to say that there is only one sun, or that the earth's sun is the center of the universe. However, the recognition of this fact does not diminish the importance of our earth's sun to us. With the improvement of knowledge and technology, the sun—the source of life and energy to mankind—has become even more important and vital to us than in the past. It has a most direct influence on our lives.

Most of the great religions, including Christianity, teach that there is only one God. Some religions even claim that their God is the true God and that the gods worshipped by other religions are false. In Buddhism, the teaching is different. Let me present you with some historical background:

More than 2500 years ago, in the land known today as Nepal, at the foot of the Himalaya mountains, there lived a prince—a human being—whose name was Siddhartha Gautama. At the age of thirty he realized the full impact of the existence of human suffering, left his palace, gave up his life of luxury, and for six years practiced many kinds of ascetic methods in search of a way to save human beings from suffering. Finally, by applying his own method of insight contemplation, he was enlightened. He was then called Buddha Shakyamuni. Buddha is a title given to one who achieves complete enlightenment; that is, one who achieves perfect wisdom and perfect compassion. He travelled to many places on the Indian continent and taught his disciples and the public for over forty-five years before he passed away at the age of eighty.

Upon enlightenment, he realized that the universe is infinite; that there are numerous worlds like the earth; and that there are numerous gods comparable to the almighty God worshipped by the people of his time.

Your attention is invited to the fact that although Buddha discovered the presence of numerous gods throughout the universe, he never tried to diminish the importance of the God worshipped by the people of his time. He simply told the truth. And that truth does not affect the importance of one specific God to a specific group of people who worship that God, because that God is still the most direct and intimate influence on that group of people.

This is the same as the discovery by the Chinese of the existence of many rulers in the world. It does not diminish the importance of the Chinese government to the Chinese. Nor does the fact that there are numerous suns in the universe diminish the importance of the earth's sun as a source of light, heat, and life itself to the earth's inhabitants.

This is the first point I wish to communicate to you: there are numerous gods in the universe, but that by no means diminishes the importance of the God worshipped by this church. In fact, a Buddhist who truly understands Buddha's teaching should respect all the gods worshipped by mankind. This explains the historical fact that no war was ever fought between believers of Buddhism and followers of other faiths. Buddhism does not have a religious sovereignty. Buddha is not a god.

The second point I wish to make is that according to Buddha's teaching, gods can be very powerful compared to human beings, but nevertheless they are not free from affliction, and can be angry. The life of a god may be very long. This explains the concept held by many religions that God is eternal. But according to Buddha the almighty God worshipped by the ancient Indians is still subject to the cycle of death and rebirth. So, a god cannot be called a buddha, i.e., an enlightened one who has freed himself from that cycle.

The third and most challenging point discovered by Buddha during his enlightenment is that every human being can become a buddha. Buddha realized that every human being possesses the same wisdom that he himself possesses, but that wisdom can be clouded by ignorance and does not easily reveal itself.

It should be emphasized that when I say every human being, I do mean that each and every one of you here can become a buddha. This is a fundamental teaching of Buddhism. To put it another way, everyone does have the potential to achieve complete wisdom and complete compassion.

Now, before explaining how one can become a buddha, let me present to you two fundamental concepts in Buddhism. One is 'samsara' and the other is 'karma.' Both words are Sanskrit, the ancient language of India. Samsara is an aspect of the universe which cannot be detected by human eyes. It is the cycle of birth and death. Buddhism teaches that the birth and death in the present lifetime of a being make only one segment in the chain of infinite lives of that being. The death of a being is by no means the end.

Buddhism further teaches that there are five kinds of life forms or existences into which a being can be reborn. The five kinds of existences are heaven-dwellers (to which gods belong), human beings, animals, hungry spirits, and hell-dwellers. After death, a human being is reborn into another existence. He or she can be reborn as a human being or, perhaps, a heaven-dweller, animal, hungry spirit, or hell-dweller. Therefore, a human being does have the opportunity to be reborn as a god in heaven. By extension, a hell-dweller can also be reborn as an animal, a human being, etc.; and a heaven-dweller can also die and be reborn as a human being, hell-dweller, and so forth. This change of existences goes on indefinitely unless and until the chain breaks, which occurs when the concept of birth and death becomes meaningless to a being. According to Buddhism, this happens when one is enlightened. Then the concept of birth and death is no longer applicable. The realization of having no birth and death is called 'nirvana,' another popular word in Sanskrit. Not only did Buddha Shakyamuni reach nirvana, many of his disciples did as well. One who achieves the status of nirvana breaks the chain of samsara and eliminates rebirth in any of the five existences. Yet, nirvana does not mean extinction.

The next question concerns who, or what, causes samsara. Who, or what, determines that the next life of a being will be in heaven or hell, or will take the form of a human being? A similar question can also be asked: Who, or what, determines that the people on this earth, although all human beings, vary so much in appearance, character, wealth, life span, health, fate, etc.? It is even more interesting to note how much the circumstances in which a person is born can influence his or her destiny. Race, nation, skin color, type of parents—all these factors make a great difference. Now, who or what determines these choices? Would it not be more logical to say that something happened before one's birth that caused all these effects, than to say that they are purely accidental, or that they are God's will? If a baby has no past life, then on what grounds would God judge whether to reward or punish that baby by causing him or her to be born under such tremendously different circumstances? According to Buddhism, it is not accidental, nor is it God's will. It is one's own actions that determine one's own destiny. Buddhism teaches that there are past, present, and future lives, and that the actions of the past have a direct effect on one's present and future lives. It should be pointed out that when I say actions of the past, it also means actions of the present, because the present is merely an instant which does not remain. As soon as we say "this is the present," it is already the past.

This law, that one's own actions determine one's own destiny, is called karma. In the Random House dictionary, karma is defined as "actions, seen as bringing upon oneself inevitable results, good or bad, either in this life or in a reincarnation." I wish to expand this definition by saying that karma is an action or combination of actions, by a being or group of beings, which produce effects. These effects, which can be good, bad, or neutral, determine the future of that being or group of beings. Good karma produces good effects; bad karma produces bad effects.*

This law of cause and effect is so powerful that it governs everything in the universe except, according to Buddhism, the one who is enlightened. Upon enlightenment, cause and effect loses its significance, and samsara ceases.

With the knowledge of samsara and karma, you may be interested to learn from Buddhism that you, as a human being, actually have the best chance to become a buddha. It may be easier to understand this if I say that the hell-dweller, the hungry spirit, and the animal have less chance to cultivate themselves and become a buddha. But why not the heaven-dweller, who is supposedly at a higher level than a human being? The answer is that life in heaven is too rich with too many pleasures. A heaven-dweller, so busy just enjoying life, has no inclination toward further cultivation. Only a human being, who has the brain capacity to receive the teachings, who has the time to practice, who has suffered hardships and sorrows that serve as alarms to stimulate one to search for a way to be rid of those sufferings, and above all, who has the opportunity to hear Buddha's teaching, possesses the ability to liberate himself and become a buddha.

It is also interesting to note that Buddhism does not encourage rebirth in heaven, but rather encourages people to follow the example of Buddha Shakyamuni, and work hard to cultivate themselves in this very life to become buddhas.

Your life may be very comfortable now. Most people living in this great country of America have a materially luxurious life, but you should not forget the fact that there are many sufferings which human beings cannot avoid. Furthermore, many people in the world are actually living in

---

*For a more detailed description of karma, see "Buddhism in Our Daily Life," Lecture 2: The Truth of Karma, pp. 53-62 below.

a condition not much better than that of hell, even without mentioning the sufferings of those in a war zone!

As I said before, suffering serves as an alarm to stimulate one to search for liberation; so let us examine the different kinds of sufferings that a human being experiences.

Eight basic sufferings were taught by Buddha 2500 years ago. At that time in India, material comfort was much less than it is today and human suffering was more noticeable. Strangely enough, however, the eight basic kinds of sufferings seem to have changed very little over the long years. These sufferings are:

suffering because of birth
suffering because of old age
suffering because of sickness
suffering because of death
suffering because of separation from loved ones
    or things one likes
suffering because of confrontation with an
    undesirable person or thing
suffering because of the denial of one's desires
suffering because of the burning intensity of the
    five aggregates of an individual (or, in simpler
    terms, the burning intensity of human
    behavior, such as hatred, jealousy, etc.)

It is regrettable that with all the progress that has brought mankind to an age when travel to other planets is imminent, human beings are still unable to lessen or abolish the basic sufferings. You may agree with me that on certain occasions suffering is even intensified by the quickening of life's pace and the increase of material temptation. This is particularly noticeable in the case of the last four kinds of sufferings.

Not only did the Buddha recognize the pervasive existence of suffering in the lives of beings, but he was also able to perceive the far-reaching significance of suffering from the broader perspective. The Buddha, with his highly developed wisdom and understanding, could see, all too clearly, that beings are trapped in the cycle of birth and

death, and thus are dominated by suffering not only in this
life but in all the innumerable lives to be experienced in
the future. He perceived the suffering that beings will experience in the future as a result of the ignorant deeds that
they are engaged in at present. Thus the Buddha's height-
ened sensitivity and insight led him to be acutely aware of
the enormous burden on sentient beings. The full extent of
this suffering is difficult to appreciate for those of us who
cannot view reality so clearly.

The realization and recognition of human suffering
is a significant step in Buddhism. It is usually referred to
as the first of the Four Noble Truths. The remaining three
Noble Truths are:

> Desire and craving are the causes of human
>   suffering;
> Suffering can be stopped; and,
> The way to stop suffering.

I have already given you too much to absorb, and time
does not permit going into the details of the Four Noble
Truths. So, I will just give you a brief explanation of the
Fourth Noble Truth, the way to stop suffering, since there
are still a few important points I wish to introduce concerning the path to take in order to become a buddha.

There are eight components which make up the way
to stop suffering. This path is usually called the Eight-fold
Right Way, and it is the guiding principle for the life of a
Buddhist. The Eight Right Ways are:

> Right View
> Right Resolve
> Right Speech
> Right Conduct
> Right Livelihood
> Right Effort
> Right Mindfulness
> Right Concentration

The key word here is 'right.' In order to make it easier
to understand its application to daily life, I define right as:

1) not hurting others and, if possible, helping others; 2) understanding the law of cause and effect (karma) and observing it carefully; and 3) understanding that your body is the vehicle on which you must rely to sail from this shore of suffering to the other shore of liberation, and so you must take care of it.

If one can live according to these guiding principles, desire and craving will decrease and suffering will thereby diminish.

Please note that Buddha's teaching pays much attention to the community and demands a high degree of self-discipline in his followers. Buddha founded the 'sangha'— an organized group of monks that conduct themselves in the right way of living. The sangha set an example for the public as to how the causes of human suffering can be controlled, reduced, and finally eliminated. Any activity or way of living which disturbs the community or creates trouble for other people, even in the name of religion, or Buddhism, should not be considered genuine Buddhism because such an activity is against Buddha's teaching.

When you study Buddhism, you will find that Buddha usually taught on two levels, depending upon the level of understanding of the audience. One level may be referred to as the enlightened level, and the other as the mundane level.

Is there anyone here who has had the experience of enlightenment or who understands Buddha's teaching on the enlightened level? I do not know. I have not. I haven't had the actual experience of enlightenment. So the little bit I'm telling you today to introduce you to the enlightened level should be treated as one tadpole repeating to another the mother frog's story about the warm sunshine and the gentle breeze she experienced on the land. The tadpole's words are not based on personal experience.

Upon enlightenment, Buddha realized that all phenomena and ideas are unreal and impermanent, arising because of human beings' incorrect and incomplete perceptions of the universe.

An example that demonstrates our incomplete perception is as follows: We human beings say that air is empty and we can freely move in it. On the other hand, water is not empty to us. However, a fish may see it entirely differently. A fish will consider water, in which he can move freely, as empty, while air is not. In fact, air may be as solid as a rock to a fish. It can hardly move an inch in air.

I can give you many other examples which all lead to the one conclusion that our eyes and ears and other sense organs do not give us a complete view of the universe, and that such incomplete information can be very misleading. Unfortunately all our knowledge, and thereby our actions, have been based entirely upon the incomplete or incorrect information perceived by our sense organs since the first instant we left our mother's womb.

Even more detrimental is the stubborn nature of our brain which refuses to accept the fact that our senses are faulty. This is because the information continuously and consistently fed into the brain by the sense organs is so incomplete. Therefore, even though you understand what I am saying at this moment, the next moment you forget or discard it completely because your eyes and ears give you an entirely different picture which your brain habitually accepts as true.

It is therefore extremely important to point out that intellectual understanding alone is not enough to overcome our habitual acceptance of this incomplete and incorrect view of the world. Enlightenment is needed. With enlightenment you can observe directly, clearly, and continuously that the universe is empty; that all phenomena and ideas are just like a dream, or like clouds floating in the sky, which come and go without leaving any trace behind. You will then be unaffected by whatever phenomena appear. Phenomena are by nature empty. They are unreal and impermanent. This is the great wisdom.

How can one become enlightened? Buddha told of his own experience, that he was enlightened by right concentration and right contemplation. You may still remember the story about the mother frog and her tadpoles I mentioned a few minutes ago. Now, I am just like the tadpole and cannot explain the experience of enlightenment to you further. But I can go on to the next point, which you have to know to become a buddha, that is, the perfection of great compassion.

To talk about great compassion, I must introduce to you one more important term in Buddhism, namely 'bodhisattva.' In Sanskrit, 'bodhi' implies enlightenment or the act of enlightening others and 'sattva' means being. So a bodhisattva is either an enlightened being or one who leads other beings to enlightenment. A bodhisattva is a being who is on the path of becoming a buddha and who is committed to helping other sentient beings reach enlightenment.

It is interesting to note that a bodhisattva can be a monk, a nun, or an ordinary person like ourselves. As a matter of fact, most of the bodhisattvas in Buddhist history were laity. This is so because to do the deeds a bodhisattva ought to do, one should be in close contact with people in the community.

The most important quality for a bodhisattva to have is compassion. Bodhisattva Avalokiteshvara (in Sanskrit), or Kuan-yin (in Chinese) is a symbolic representative of great compassion. The great vow of this bodhisattva was to free all sentient beings from fears of any kind. Allow me to quote two sentences of a famous verse:

> I shall go to thousands of places
> In response to the thousands of prayers.
> In the vast sea of suffering,
> I always serve as a ferry to deliver beings.

In this verse you may note that there is

1) no geographical limitation
2) no limit to the number of prayers to which the bodhisattva will respond
3) no restriction as to what kind of prayers will receive responses
4) no discrimination as to who is making the prayer
5) no interruption in serving; it continues day and night
6) no expectation of a reward of any kind

This is the great compassion one should learn.

At this point you may think that this is quite similar to the 'great love' taught by Christ. And rightly so, because according to a Buddhist interpretation, Jesus Christ was indeed a great bodhisattva. On many occasions Christ taught his followers to give totally of themselves in the service of others. He himself even gave his own life.

Thank you very much.

BUDDHISM IN OUR DAILY LIFE

A series of lectures delivered at
The China Institute in America
New York, New York
1976

Lecture 1:

THE CONCEPT OF BIRTH AND DEATH

Dear friends:

In the Christian Bible, in the Book of John, chapter XVI, verse 12, Jesus Christ tells his disciples, "I have yet many things to say unto ye, but ye cannot bear them now." It seems that what Christ did teach his disciples was only a part of what he knew, perhaps because of the level of understanding of his disciples at that time. Unfortunately, Jesus died at the age of thirty-three. Time did not allow him to give his disciples a complete course of teaching. What Christ knew but did not say remains an unanswerable question.

On the other hand, Buddha lived for eighty years. He had forty-five full years after his enlightenment to teach his disciples; long enough to gradually lead them to learn and practice various stages of teaching, starting with a self-centered liberation from human suffering, eventually reaching the most profound supramundane doctrine.

If we can assume that the founders of two of the greatest religions on earth were both persons possessed of profound wisdom, then many teachings expounded by Buddha could have been those known by Christ but which he lacked the time to teach.

With this in mind, it seems to me that the study of Buddhism by Christians can have a special significance, that is, the search for what Christ knew but did not say.

The Buddhist concept of birth and death could be a good example of just such an area of thought. For this reason, I have introduced this talk with some reflections about the teachings of Christ.

Now, let me move to the mysterious question which has occupied the human mind for thousands of years: "What happens to us after the so-called experience of death?"

Practically all systems of political and philosophical thought deal only with the living. For example, as Confucius said, "We do not even know the living, how can we know the dead?" From the practical point of view, it is true that problems concerning the living are more important and relevant to us. However, this approach evades a real answer to my question. The fact of death, and the question as to what happens afterward, remain. In fact, it could well be that our attitude toward living could change greatly if we knew what happened after death.

It should be noted that Confucius did not say that death is extinction, nor did he say that there is no future life after death. He simply meant that to live as a decent person on earth is more important than to question the nature of life after death.

Most religions, however, do have a teaching on life after death. Two teachings about death predominate among world religions: one is the one-life theory and the other is the multi-life theory. Christianity is one of the religions that teaches the one-life theory. According to this teaching, the life of a physical body begins at birth, but there is also a spiritual entity called the 'soul' abiding in that body. Death is the destruction of the body, but not of the soul. After death, the soul, depending upon the judgement of the Creator, will ascend to heaven or descend to hell. The implication is that each person has only this one life on earth and will eventually remain eternally, either blissfully in heaven, or suffering in hell, with no chance of ever leaving. Whether or not this implication represents a complete understanding of Christ's teaching is unclear. It could be that Christ had much more to teach about birth and death, but did not have time to bring his students to a higher level of understanding.

The multi-life theory says that the birth and death of a being is only one segment in the chain of infinite lives of that being. In various lives the being wanders among five major kinds of existence. The five existences are: heaven-dweller, human being, animal, hungry spirit, and hell-dweller. After death a human being is reborn into a new existence. He or she could be a human being again, or perhaps a heaven-dweller, or an animal or a hungry spirit, or a hell-dweller. Similarly, a dweller in hell can also be reborn as an animal, a human being, etc., and a heaven- dweller also dies and is reborn as a human being, or hell- dweller, and so forth. This change of life form, or existence, goes on indefinitely until and unless the chain breaks, which occurs when the concept of birth and death is no longer significant to a being.

Hinduism and Buddhism hold this multi-life theory, but with a major difference in their views on how the chain is broken. Hinduism sustains the belief that the concept of birth and death becomes insignificant when the being is merged with Brahman—Almighty God. Buddhism says that it becomes insignificant upon enlightenment, when the concept of birth and death is no longer applicable.

To understand the Buddhist concept, we must first understand that Buddhism explains world phenomena at two levels. The first is the enlightened level, that is, the level at which the ultimate truth is realized. The other is the mundane level, which can be further divided into the intellectual level, where most of us here find ourselves, and the common level, to which the majority of people on earth belong.

At the enlightened level, the concept of birth and death is no longer applicable. I shall explain this later. At the mundane level, however, Buddhism holds the multi-life theory and recognizes the individuality of a being, which can then be compared with the soul as taught in Christianity and Hinduism. In Buddhism, the individuality of a being is described as a stream, in which each moment is caused by the previous. The example is given of a string of beads, the movement of each bead determining that of the next. The important point, however, is that there is no string running through these beads; no permanent entity beyond the path of cause and effect.

Thus, in Buddhism the continuation of individuality does not mean that a physical body is transported into the next life, or that everything stored in one's brain (which is also part of the physical body) will pass into the next life. As a matter of fact, the physical body changes from moment to moment. Just look at the photographs taken some time ago and you will agree with me. What does pass into the next life or future lives, and constitutes the continuation of individuality, is the force of the effects of one's actions in this present life and in previous lives. This is called, in both Buddhism and Hinduism, the law of karma. I shall explain this principle in my next talk.

At this point you might like to say, "That is fine, but 1) please show me where heaven and hell may be found, and 2) please prove to me that I existed before my birth and will still be in existence after my death."

To answer the first question, may I ask, "Do you believe that your own eyes are capable of seeing heaven or hell?" If someone did show us heaven or hell, would we not say that it was just a hallucination, or magic, and therefore not believe it? If you have studied the electromagnetic spectrum, you may agree with me that our human eyes can only see an infinitesimal part of the universe, and that there are so many things our eyes cannot see.* A few hundred years ago, no one could see the whole bone structure of a living

*See "The Five Eyes," p. 1 et seq. above.

human body, but now we can see it by means of x-rays. We are advancing very rapidly into the microscopic universe and also into outer space. Who knows? Maybe in a number of years from now, a new detective instrument will be invented that will enable human beings to see a different wave length from the presently visible light wave, and human beings may discover that the so-called hell is right here on earth; or, space instruments will send back some pictures of outer space that could turn out to be one of the heavens or worlds postulated by Buddha.

With respect to the second question, sporadic records all over the world indicate that ordinary people have remembered past lives, or that others, like certain high Tibetan lamas, could predict where they would be reborn. But all of these reports do not present enough scientific evidence to convince us conclusively that rebirth does exist.

I am, therefore, using another approach to see if there are some phenomena in our universe that can explain the concept of birth and death, and that may give some clues to this mysterious question. The simple reason which convinced me that this approach has merit is the fact that we human beings are no more than a product of nature and are entirely governed by natural laws such as gravitational force. Therefore, the laws that characterize other natural phenomena may very well be applicable to human beings.

As I study this question, interestingly enough, I find a number of phenomena in the universe which provide good analogies to the multi-life theory of human existence. The simplest and easiest for us to comprehend are the multiforms of H_2O.

Do we all know H_2O? Yes.

H_2O is the chemical formula for water, signifying two parts of hydrogen to one part of oxygen. The chemical formula H_2O does not change when water turns into vapor at the boiling point or into ice at the freezing point. Nor is H_2O different when it appears in the beautiful, white, crystalized form to which people give the name of snow; or in the minute liquid particles suspended in the air that are called fog.

Now a very interesting concept arises. Water disappears when it is changed into vapor or ice. Would you not say that at that very moment, water is dead and vapor or ice is born? Or when snow melts and becomes water, would you not say that at that instant, the snow is dead and water is born? This would be true when water is identified simply as water. However, if water is not identified only as water, but also as H_2O, then the concept of birth and death does not apply. H_2O remains unchanged when its appearance changes from water to vapor or ice or vice versa. H_2O has not really undergone "death and rebirth," although its appearance and physical characteristics may have changed an infinite number of times and people may have given it many different names. Nor will H_2O undergo death and rebirth in the future, although its appearance and physical characteristics will change numerous times, until H_2O finally disintegrates into hydrogen and oxygen (which phenomenon I will explain later.)

From this analogy we can see that the multi-life theory as suggested by Hinduism and Buddhism makes more sense and could be closer to the truth than might have been apparent at first. I therefore draw the following conclusions:

1) We can postulate that there is something in the universe equivalent to H_2O and its various manifestations, which I will refer to as 'X.' X manifests as various types of beings, i.e., the heaven-dwellers, human beings, animals, hungry spirits, and hell-dwellers. In Christianity and Hinduism, X is called the soul. In Buddhism, at the mundane level, X can also be called the soul.

2) The five forms of existence are interchangeable. Thus, a human being can be reborn as a heaven-dweller, a hungry spirit, an animal, or a hell-dweller. A heaven-dweller can be reborn as a human being, an animal, a hungry spirit, or a hell-dweller. By the same token, a hell-dweller can also be reborn into other forms, including that of a human being.

3) According to Buddhism, one cannot live in heaven eternally, nor will one stay in hell indefinitely. Life goes on, its form changing continuously. This phenomenon of the continuous flow of death and rebirth among the five existences is called samsara.

4) The concept of birth and death is only meaningful if one refers to a specific object. If the reference is shifted to the more fundamental nature of that object, the concept of birth and death is not applicable. Water and H_2O are an example: water is the specific object, H_2O the more fundamental level. A golden ring, which is a specific object, and the raw gold, which is a more basic material, is another good example.

5) This is important: If one identifies oneself as a human being, then one does undergo death and rebirth. The same applies to water if water is identified as water, or a golden ring if it is identified as a golden ring. But, if one identifies oneself as X, then there is no death, even when the form of X appearing as a human being is destroyed. From the point of view of X, there is only a continuous change of form, while X remains unchanged. Again, the same applies if water is identified as H_2O or a golden ring as gold. Therefore, if we wish to be rid of death, or samsara, the first thing we should do is to avoid identifying ourselves as human beings. Unfortunately, this goes entirely against our will. We are strongly attached to our identity as human beings and that is why we are in samsara.

Now the basic purpose of Buddha's teaching is to enable beings to remove themselves from samsara. Therefore, the essence of Buddhism is to teach how one can identify oneself with X. Furthermore, an important point is that Buddhism does not teach us to treat X as the soul. The soul is not ultimate; it is still subject to death, just as H_2O is subject to disintegration into hydrogen and oxygen. Buddhism teaches us to identify ourselves with the X as interpreted at the enlightened level. At the enlightened level we are told that X is something incomprehensible to the human mind and that it can only be realized and recognized by the enlightened consciousness. But if that is so, then how can we comprehend and explain it? Luckily, in modern science I do find something that can probably help us immensely to understand the interpretation of X at the enlightened level. This is energy.

In modern science we learn that everything in the

universe is a form of energy. Electricity, heat, light, fire, sound, chemical reaction, matter, all are different manifestations of energy. Energy itself cannot be seen, heard, smelled, tasted, or touched, but all over the universe its manifested forms, infinite in number, can be seen, heard, smelled, tasted, touched, or otherwise detected by human organs. Energy, therefore, can be considered as the universal ultimate. It should be noted, however that energy is only a name arbitrarily chosen by human beings. The definition of energy has, in fact, been modified since the word was first used. So please do not adhere strictly to the dictionary's definition of the word. I may interpret the word differently than do some scientists. The word energy, as I use it here, is given to something in the universe that comprises the entire universe, and cannot be seen, heard, smelled, tasted, or touched by human organs, but can manifest itself in numerous forms that can be detected by the senses. Since it fully comprises the entire universe, it cannot be increased or decreased; it has no motion. In short, energy is the universe and the universe is energy.

If you are able to comprehend what I have described above as energy, then you should have less difficulty in understanding X as explained in Buddhism at the enlightened level. Upon enlightenment, according to Buddhism, one realizes that one's X, and only that X, comprises the entire universe; that X is the universe and the universe is X; that X cannot be increased or decreased; that X has no motion, and that X can be neither defiled nor purified. Because X is so difficult to explain and to comprehend, Buddhists, for over 2,500 years, have given it many different names, in the attempt to clarify the concept. The simplest term, in my opinion, is 'basic nature.' The word 'basic' signifies that all world phenomena are derived from it, rather than being separate. Unlike the concept of soul, basic nature implies no isolation of the individual. There can be no other entity. This X is me, you, everyone, and everything. Therefore how can X die? How can the concept of death and rebirth be applicable to X? This basic nature, therefore, is what one should identify with.

On the other hand, Buddhism makes it clear that unless one is enlightened and one's basic nature is manifest, one is always subject to the chain of endless death and rebirth that is samsara. Buddhism, therefore, is a teaching that we should look into seriously, because it provides the means for us to realize and recognize our basic nature. In this way we can rid ourselves of the endless and uncontrollable death and rebirth, which is the source of all suffering.

I also wish to emphasize, however, that in our daily life the multi-life theory is even more important than the enlightened vision of X, because we all are not enlightened and are still subject to samsara. It would be a terrible mistake to neglect this multi-life theory and simply think, "I am the universe and there is no death," for when death comes, one will still be horrified.

As a conclusion to today's talk, I wish to introduce the following views on two of the most important sociological phenomena in our daily lives:

1) Killing does not mean the elimination of an opponent and the achievement of victory, as one usually thinks. On the contrary, since only the physical human form is destroyed, the victim still exists. It is therefore not a victory, and it could be the beginning of many troubles.

2) Suicide does not mean the end of suffering. The physical human form may be destroyed, but life goes on. The problem could become much more complicated and serious as a result of killing the self.

Thus I have said at the beginning of this talk that the attitude of the living could change very much if we knew what happened after the so-called death that we observe. Political scientists, politicians, and philosophers who ignore this important question could be making a serious error out of short-sightedness. We look into this subject more penetratingly in the following talk, "The Truth of Karma."

Lecture 2:

THE TRUTH OF KARMA

Dear friends:

In last week's discussion of the concept of birth and death, the one-life and the multi-life theories were introduced. I also used a familiar natural phenomenon, the multiform of H_2O, to illustrate my belief that the multi-life theory taught by Hinduism and Buddhism is closer to the truth than is the one-life theory. We found that H_2O is a good analogy for the human soul.

Then, we observed that H_2O is not the ultimate substance of the universe. Modern science is gradually concluding that energy could be that ultimate substance. This agrees with Buddha's teaching that the soul is not the ultimate nature of a human being. Rather, the ultimate nature is something which is incomprehensible; without duality, boundary, or birth and death, and with no difference from the universe. 'Basic nature,' 'original nature,' and 'buddha-nature' are some of the names given to this ultimate quality. The famous statement made by Buddha upon his enlightenment was "Every sentient being has buddha-nature."

The vast, boundless, and empty space is usually used as an analogy to basic nature, to signify its lack of duality and discrimination, and its limitlessness in both time and space. Since the ultimate existence of a human being is such, the concept of birth and death becomes inapplicable when one is enlightened or when one recognizes one's basic nature. But since most of us have not been enlightened, it does not help us too much to discuss basic nature at this stage. We first have to establish a clear understanding of the multi-life theory at the mundane level, which directly affects our daily lives.

To appreciate thoroughly the multi-life theory, one must first answer an important question: What causes the change from one form of existence, say, a human being, to another form, say, an animal?

To help us understand this it is useful to refer to the H_2O model again. Let us first examine the causes of changes in the forms of H_2O, from water to vapor, or ice to water.

From physics we learn the following chain of causation:

| physical or chemical action | $\rightarrow$ | intangible form of energy called heat | $\rightarrow$ | change of intensity or activity of H_2O molecules | $\rightarrow$ | change in form of H_2O |

This illustration is quite obvious and needs no explanation. I will just give you a few examples of physical and chemical actions and you will instantly know that these are the causes of water, vapor, snow, ice, or other forms of H_2O. Such actions as radiation from the sun, the setting of a fire, the passing of electricity through metallic wires, and the dissolving of chemicals in water are all familiar examples of processes that produce heat and ultimately change the form of H_2O.

According to Buddhism, a similar natural phenomenon is going on in the universe: that is, the various actions carried out by a being in the past and present which produce a kind of intangible force that causes the being to change from one form of existence to another. That is why we have the different forms of heaven-dweller, human being, animal, hungry spirit, and hell-dweller. These various existences constitute samsara, or the continuous round of life and death.

In Hinduism and Buddhism, such actions bear a common name—karma. Karma means an action, or combination of actions, by a single being or group of beings which produce effects. Those effects, which could be good, bad, or neutral, determine the future of the being who performed the action. Karmic actions, therefore, are the heart of the multi-life theory, just as physical and chemical actions are the basic causes of the multi-forms of H_2O.

I would like to illustrate this comparison of the above-mentioned analogies:

physical or chemical actions	→	intangible form of energy called heat	→	change of intensity or activity of H_2O molecules	→	change in form of H_2O
karma	→	intangible force called the karmic force	→	good, bad, or neutral effects upon activities of the being	→	change in the form of the being = samsara

This concept of karma plays a very important role throughout Asia. Asian religions in general have established the famous universal moral code based upon this law, that good deeds produce good effects and bad deeds produce bad effects. However, it should be pointed out that Buddhism places additional qualifications on this code:

1) The so-called good effect or bad effect is not a judgment nor is it given as a reward or punishment by a supramundane authority such as God. The good or bad effect produced by good or bad karma is purely and simply a natural phenomenon governed by natural laws that act automatically, with complete justice. If God has anything to do with it, then God must also act according to this natural law. This cause produces this effect. That cause produces that effect. God would not change this natural path because of his like or dislike of a particular person.

2) The good and bad referred to here are not defined by any code or law created by human beings unless such a code or law follows the natural path. For example, when

democracy was first established in the United States, women did not have the right to vote. At that time, women who complied with that status were considered good and those who fought against it were considered bad. That judgment was incorrect, however. The natural path is that human beings are all equal, and thus the system which gives women equal voting rights with men is truly the just one. Therefore, those who opposed the unequal voting system were actually the good ones.

This law of karma, or cause and effect, is so powerful that it governs everything in the universe except, according to Buddhism, the one who is enlightened or who recognizes basic nature. Upon enlightenment, the round of cause and effect loses its significance, just as samsara, or the round of birth and death, ceases with enlightenment. Since basic nature transcends all duality and is ultimate, there is no one to receive the effect, whether it is good or bad, and no one to whom any effect can apply. This unique explanation by Buddha of the nullification of the law of karma is very important. I will discuss it below.

With this brief explanation of karma as a background, let us now go a step further to see how karma works.

1) Karmic effects determine rebirth.

In Buddhist texts one finds numerous discussions on what cause produces what effect. Generally speaking, the karma of present and past lives determines the form of existence in the next life. We may outline these karmic effects as follows:

a) Such karma as honesty, generosity, kindness, compassion, the relieving of others' suffering, or the creation of major benefits for others may produce the effect of being reborn in heaven.

b) Karma such as giving generously to the needy, aiding those in difficulty, making offerings to the Buddha, Dharma, and Sangha or saints in other religions, or giving others knowledge or skills that will improve their way of life, may cause one to be reborn as a human being with a wealthy and bright future.

c) Karma such as saving others' lives, refraining from killing, relieving others' worries, curing others' illnesses, generously helping hospitals and medical research, or aiding environmental improvement may cause one to be reborn as a human being with a long life and good health, a person liked and supported by many people.

d) The karma of studying the Dharma, introducing right knowledge to others by means of teaching or writing, giving sincere respect to Buddha, Dharma, and Sangha and the saints in other religions, or meditating on the mind can produce the effect of being reborn as a human being with wisdom, intelligence, eloquence in speech, and the qualities of a good scholar.

e) Despite such karma as killing, hunting, fishing, doing harm to others, endangering others' lives, manufacturing or trading weapons, or robbing, one may be born as a human being again, but with the possibility of a short lifespan, accidental death, frightening insanity, disastrous illness, etc. Further, if those negative activities were dominant in the being's life, then the rebirth will be in the form of an animal or hungry spirit or even a hell-dweller.

In one of the Buddhist texts it is recorded that someone asked Buddha:

Why are some women ugly but rich?
Why are some women beautiful but poor?
Why are some people poor but with good health
and a long life?
Why are some rich yet ill and short-lived?

The Buddha's answers were:
One who is ugly but rich was short-tempered in past lives—easily irritated and angered—but was also very generous and gave offerings to the Buddha, Dharma, and Sangha and made contributions to many sentient beings.

One who is beautiful but poor was, in past lives, very kind, always smiling and soft spoken, but was stingy and reluctant to make offerings or help other people.

The person who is poor but in good health and enjoying a long life was, in his or her past lives, very stingy or reluctant to make donations, but was kind to all sentient beings, did not harm or kill others, and also saved many sentient beings' lives.

The person who is rich but often ill, or who is short-lived, was, in his or her past lives, very generous in helping others but loved hunting and killing and caused sentient beings to feel worried, insecure, and frightened.

The above examples give us some idea of why people on earth, although all human beings, vary so much in appearance, character, lifespan, health, mental ability, and fate. It is even more interesting to note how much the circumstances in which a person is born can influence his or her destiny. Which race, which nation, which skin color, which era—all these factors make a great difference. Would it not be more logical to think that something was going on before one's birth that caused all those effects than to say that it is purely accidental or even to say that it is God's will? If a baby has no past life, then on what grounds does God judge whether to reward or to punish that baby by causing him or her to be born under different circumstances?

2) One's karma also affects others and produces effects in the present lifetime as well as in future lives.

"Karmic effect is incomprehensible!" This statement of Buddha suggests not only the complexity of karmic effects but also the difficulty of predicting when a karmic effect will mature.

Generally speaking, however, karma is like the action of lighting a candle. The candle will light the whole room immediately and will last until it is consumed. Similarly, karma has the following characteristics:

a) Karma not only affects the doer but also affects others. The magnitude of the karma determines the sphere of its effect.

b) Most karma produces an immediate effect which will last until it is consumed. The nature and magnitude of a karmic action determine the duration of the effect, which may remain many years, or may not even be felt until some other karmic conditions mature.

c) Karmic effects can combine and accumulate.

These three points are rather condensed. I do not have time to give you a detailed description of them. The following examples however, might help you to understand these points a bit more:

a) The discovery of electricity by Benjamin Franklin and the conversion of electricity into light by Thomas Edison changed the lives of human beings tremendously, and the effect is still growing.

b) An action taken by the U.S. Congress to change the tax law will immediately affect millions of American pockets. The effect can be seen by many Americans in their lifetime, and it will also be felt by future generations of Americans.

c) The combined and cumulative karma of the system of slavery used by many Americans over a long period of time has produced effects which constitute a major domestic problem in the U.S.

d) The theoretical discovery of atomic energy by Albert Einstein and the joint effort of all the participants in the Manhattan Project produced such complicated effects, good and bad, that we are probably just beginning to realize the significance of these developments.

3) A comparison can be made of the magnitude of effects of various kinds of karma.

Such comparisons are recorded in many Buddhist scriptures. I would like to give you some examples to enable you to form your own ideas on how you may create karmic effects of greater magnitude.

a) One day, while walking on the street, Buddha met a beggar who was a so-called untouchable in the strict caste society of India during his time. Not only was Buddha friendly with him, but he accepted the beggar as a disciple in his order of the Sangha. This action had an effect which was infinitely greater than the acceptance of a prince as his disciple.

b) When the monk Bodhidharma went from India to China he was welcomed by Emperor Liang. The emperor asked him, "What merit have I gained since I built so many temples, erected so many pagodas, made so many offerings to Buddha, Dharma, and Sangha, and did numerous other virtuous deeds?" Bodhidharma's reply greatly disappointed Emperor Liang. Bodhidharma said, "Your Majesty, there is none. You have gained no merit. What you have done produces only worldly rewards, that is, good fortune, great power, or great wealth in your future lives, but you will still be wandering around in samsara."

c) Buddha often emphasized that to study and explain to others even a few sentences of the teachings that show how to be rid of samsara creates infinitely greater merit than making tremendous offerings to as many Buddhas all over the universe as there are grains of sand in the great Ganges River.

d) Buddha also taught these principles:

One who makes numerous offerings to the Buddha, Dharma, and Sangha, helps sentient beings, and does many good deeds, and yet dedicates all the merit accumulated thereby to one's own or one's relatives' interest such as making more money or enjoying a longer or better present or future life produces limited effects.

One who does those same good deeds but dedicates all the merit to saving sentient beings from suffering in samsara receives much greater merit than the one with selfish purposes.

Finally, one who does the same good deeds with no specific purpose or desire at all receives infinitely greater merit than the two cases mentioned above.

4) Karma and free will.

This topic has been discussed often. The question is: "Is there any room for free will under the law of karma?" A more penetrating question is: "Might not free will be simply subjective opinion? So-called free will is also an effect of karma." For example, suppose a daughter goes against her parents' wishes and decides to marry a younger man. The daughter might think that the decision was made by her free will, but under the law of karma that decision could very well be an effect of her past karmic relation with this young man and her parents. That she acts with a free will is only her subjective opinion.

In the United States, people have the freedom to vote or not to vote. Is this freedom obtained by a kind of free will or is it predetermined by karmic effect?

We could find many examples, all of which seem to indicate that there is no room for free will under the law of karma. Does this mean the fate of a person is predetermined by his or her past karma, that a person has no way to change it? Buddha said this is not the case. Why and how, then, can one change one's fate?

To help you to understand that one's fate is not entirely predetermined by one's past karma, I must ask you to recall what I said before about our basic nature. Cause and effect, just like birth and death, lose their significance at the enlightened level because at the level of basic nature there is no one to receive the effect of karma, whether it is good or bad. Therefore, at the extreme, when one is enlightened, the law of karma is not applicable. All that the enlightened one does, says, or thinks is through free will, a manifestation of basic nature, and not the effect of past karma.

All of Buddha's teachings aim at this one goal: that is, to identify oneself with one's basic nature. All his methods are designed to enable one to gradually come into harmony with that basic nature.

Now, basic nature possesses all kinds of good human qualitites, such as loving-kindness, compassion, joy, and equanimity. All these good qualities could cause good karma, which produces good effects. Therefore, during the process of cultivating harmony with basic nature, these good qualities will be revealed bit by bit, like an occasional ray of sunshine penetrating through a heavy cloud. These revelations are the true products of a person's free will. Because such free will creates good karma, and because good karma produces good effects which in turn are good karma for the next effect, and so on, a person has the potential to become enlightened, to recognize basic nature, and to become a Buddha.

One will thus not only be rid of samsara, but will also gain the perfect wisdom and compassion necessary to teach other sentient beings to follow the same path.

Karma is such a vast subject that I could talk for hours without exhausting the material. Topics like the following could be very interesting:

1)   Can good karma and bad karma offset each other?
2)   Can karma be erased?
3)   Can the effects of bad karma be minimized by confession or other kinds of repentance?

With the general idea of karma I have presented to you today, you may be able to find the answers to those questions.

In conclusion, I wish to emphasize two points:

1) Good or bad karma will inevitably produce its respective effect. Our daily doings, speech, and thoughts will affect our future. A wise person knows, therefore, how to live properly.

2) Remember that the law of karma stops operating and you become rid of samsara only by identifying yourself with your basic nature. How you may gradually identify yourself with basic nature, and realize that it is yourself, is the essence of Buddha's teaching. I sincerely recommend that you study and practice it.

Among all the hindrances to our cultivation of enlightenment, the greatest obstacle is our concept of self. This is the core of all our ignorance and suffering. Next week, we shall attack that core. I can assure you that it is indeed very, very hard.

Lecture 3:

THE TRUTH OF SELF (EMPTINESS)

Dear friends:

Someone asked me why I used the word 'emptiness' in parenthesis after the word 'self' in the title of this talk. According to Buddhism, the answer is that "self is emptiness and emptiness is self." This answer, however, is too simple to comprehend. So before I explain the subject matter of this title, let me make two remarks:

1) Emptiness or void, as used in Buddhism, does not mean nothingness, as in "the room was empty after all the people left." It means, actually, that the basic nature of everything is emptiness. Even if the room is packed with people, it should still be envisioned as empty. However, human language often is not adequate to convey such precise expression. The word 'emptiness' appeared to be closest in meaning to the Sanskrit 'shunyata,' and so it was chosen by the English-speaking scholars who first came into contact with Buddhism. The word does create confusion, but there is no other suitable term in the English vocabulary.

2) Although the truth discovered by the Buddha upon his enlightenment was incomprehensible to ordinary human minds, he had to rely on the language understandable to people. Buddha's teaching was therefore delivered at two different levels: the mundane level and the enlightened level. At the mundane level, the concept of self means there is an individual. At the enlightened level, however, 'individual,' 'non-individual,' 'self,' 'non-self,' 'phenomenon,' 'no phenom-

enon,' 'name,' and 'no name' are all merely sophisms. At the
enlightened level, one envisions all people, including oneself, as those seen in a dream or appearing on a television
screen. Such visions are empty. Even the term 'emptiness'
is unnecessary and carries no real meaning. 'Emptiness' is
just arbitrarily chosen for convenience of discussion among
people at the mundane level.

The concept of self at the mundane level, nevertheless, is the biggest hindrance to ordinary people in achieving
enlightenment. To put it another way, one cannot achieve
enlightenment and identify with basic nature without first
achieving the realization that the concept of self is not only
an invalid concept, but also a dangerous concept. With the
concept of self the concept of 'that is mine' is also established,
and thus the attachments of both self and 'that is mine'
become firmly planted in one's mind. In this way one can
never be in harmony with basic nature, one can never achieve
enlightenment and be rid of samsara, the recurring cycle
of birth and death, which is the source of suffering.

In today's talk, I would like to explain first how the
concept of self is formed and strengthened. Next, I shall try
to explore, using several different approaches, how this concept of self is invalid. By destruction of the concept of self,
the concept of emptiness will be formed. The concept of emptiness is also an attachment. Thus we should finally destroy
the concept of emptiness, to enable our true basic nature to
be revealed.

The concept of self has been deeply rooted in our minds
for so long that it is unrealistic to expect that it can be
eliminated by the time we walk out of this room. It is my
hope that after listening to this lecture your concept of self
will simply not be strengthed further, and that this lecture
will provide you with some leads useful for your future
development.

According to Buddhism, the concept of self has two
major components: one is the desire for unending life or
continuous existence, and the other is the attachment to
one's own view, usually expressed as 'my view.' The desire
for continuous existence is present even before birth. The
attachment to one's own view is gradually built up during

one's lifetime, although such views are largely influenced by one's past karma.

The concept of self is first conceived through one's sensory organs. Through them one establishes oneself, even at birth, as a physical body which is separate from the so-called outside world. This concept of self becomes stronger and more important as one grows up. As a result, one finds that one has established within one's physical body a center of awareness, the self, with respect to the outside world.

Secondly, because everyone is establishing his or her own center of activity, the perception that the world is composed of different entities is further sharpened. Since each entity seeks its own satisfaction, conflicts of interest develop. The feeling of separation is further compounded when views differ and each entity asserts the importance or rightness of its own view.

Voluminous Buddhist commentaries have been written on the subject of the development of the concept of self. What I've just said here is comparable to a drop of water in the vast ocean. However, the ocean, as vast as it is, is basically just water. So, if we can study this drop of water thoroughly, a good foundation will be built for a more advanced study of the ocean later on.

The physical body of a person is the core upon which the concept of self is imposed. However, the concept of self is further strengthened by all sorts of identifications made in daily life which increase one's separation and isolation from others in the outside world. Some of the most common phenomena by which one identifies oneself and which distinguish one person from another are:

1) name
2) appearance
3) voice
4) fingerprint
5) sensation
6) ideology
7) reputation

These identifications are like the branches and leaves of a tree, with the physical human body as its root. If the root is dug out, then all the leaves and branches will automatically pass out of existence.

The above statement has, nevertheless, been challenged by a friend of mine who is a forester. He said to me, "Since you have not had the experience of taking down a big tree, you do not know that the branches should be cut off first, then the trunk cut down, and finally the root dug out or pulverized." I certainly could not argue with him; however, I told him that in Buddhism there are three major paths which teach a variety of ways for human beings to dig out the root of the concept of self. These three paths are:

> Path 1—Vigorous practice, with the goal of destroying all the habits one has accumulated during this life and also during past lives. Such habits even include knowledge, faith, love, and hatred, and all kinds of human activities. Ch'an (pronounced Zen in Japanese) and the teachings of the Tibetan enlightened one, Milarepa, belong to this path. It is analogous to the idea of concentrating one's efforts on digging out the root without cutting off the branches first.

> Path 2—Reliance upon the law of karma, whereby the concept of self can be gradually eliminated and basic nature revealed through the accumulation of merit gained by practicing the six perfections (paramitas). These are perfection of giving (dana paramita), perfection of moral discipline (shila paramita), perfection of patience (kshanti paramita), perfection of energetic perserverance (virya paramita), perfection of meditation (dhyana paramita), and perfection of wisdom (prajna paramita). This path is analogous to the standard forestry method of first cutting off the branches and trunk, and finally removing the root.

Paths 1 and 2 are methods of cultivation, but without a sound theoretical foundation, people can go astray on Path 1, or may lose enthusiasm after a period of time on Path 2. We therefore also need Path 3.

> Path 3—Establishment of the theoretical foundation for Paths 1 and 2 through learning and penetrative reasoning.

In this lecture I regret that I am able to introduce to you only very little from each path. Today let us follow Path 3 to see how the concept of self can be theoretically destroyed so that our basic nature can be revealed. The next talk will be devoted to Paths 1 and 2, but also very briefly and with regard to selected topics only.

Now, let us first examine the seven means of identification that I mentioned above, to see how these branches of the "tree of self" can be removed.

1) A name is probably the most common way of identifying a person, but it is obvious that it is a poor means of doing so. Not only can a name be changed, but many people have the same name. Thus, that branch can easily be cut off. A name cannot really separate one person from the other.

2) Appearance, including the form of the body, complexion, color, etc., is also commonly used to identify a person. But not only does appearance change with age, it can also be changed by surgery. It may serve a temporary purpose, but it cannot really be used to establish the concept of self.

3) Scientific experiments demonstrate that each person has a different voice pattern. An instrument has even been devised by which a court may identify a person by his vocal pattern. But physical damage to the vocal apparatus can change that pattern, and certainly this means of identification is not applicable to mutes. Voice, therefore, also cannot permanently separate one person from another such that each person could justifiably be called a self.

4) Fingerprints are commonly used to identify a person but, like the voice, are not perfect. One does not lose one's concept of self even if one cuts off both of one's hands.

5) It is true that sensation, such as pain, delight, and the apprehension of danger, does alert one to the existence of a self, but such alertness is usually temporary and simply affirms the concept of self which one has already.

6) Ideology is a powerful means of identification. It is, in fact, part of the premise of one's so-called view, which is one of the two main components that form the self. Historians have recorded that many religious defenders and re-

volutionaries put their ideas, faith, or principles even above their lives. Although in those cases the concept of self as an individual is usually surrendered to the concept of self as a group, the concept of self is, nevertheless, strengthened. But ideology can be changed, and a change in one's ideology does not mean a change in the individual. The concept of self remains. Thus it can be proven that ideology is still not the core of the concept of self.

7) Reputation is also a strong identification of self. Reputation represents one's deeds, which distinguish one from other persons. Reputation can be planted very deeply in one's mind. It is not surprising to learn that one of the presidents of the United States heard people call him "Mr. President" in his dreams. Ego is a term which represents a person's strong attachment to his identification by reputation. Pride and arrogance are usually the by-products. Just like ideology, however, fame can change overnight. The destruction of one's reputation does not, unfortunately, mean the destruction of the self. Thus this branch, one's reputation, can also be removed without affecting the concept of self.

With all branches cut off we now face the root of the tree of self, that is, the reality of the human body.

More than 2,000 years ago a famous Chinese philosopher, Lao-Tzu, remarked, "My biggest problem is that I have a body." Buddha also emphasized that the body is the source of all human suffering. So, we go to the core of the problem. Can the human body justifiably be called the self?

In a previous talk, "The Five Eyes," I have studied this important and fundamental question, by employing three analytical methods taught by Buddha.* Each of these methods leads to the conclusion that the physical human body is a manifestation of emptiness (shunyata) and that the term 'self' is just a name arbitrarily chosen by human beings for the convenience of living in this world.

Since we can show that the physical human body is impermanent and is a momentarily changeable form seen

_____
*See above, p. 5 et seq.

by human eyes in a very narrow range of wave lengths, how is it justifiable to call it a self, an individual entity? Thus we can conclude that there is no self, only emptiness.

Once I introduced this doctrine of "no self, only emptiness" to some of my friends. One friend cried, "If I lose myself and become emptiness, how can I still be alive?" To this question I answered, "The Buddha reached the realization that there is no self, only emptiness, upon his enlightenment at the age of thirty-five, yet he lived a happy life until he was eighty years old." The destruction of the concept of self, and the understanding of emptiness, do not mean the end of life; on the contrary, these realizations mark the beginning of a happy life. I will discuss this more fully in the next talk.

Lecture 4:

THE SOURCE OF JOY

Dear friends:

Let me make it clear, first of all, that the joy I refer to here is not the temporary joy that can be the cause or source of later suffering. For example, one does have a sensation of joy and being carefree when one is drunk. But the actions one might commit while intoxicated could be so foolish that one might feel deep regret afterward, or they could cause such irreparable damage that the suffering created thereby would be much greater and longer lasting than the temporary joy that accompanied the drinking. That kind of joy, if you still wish to call it joy, is classified in Buddhism as suffering—it is not joy, because it is the beginning of suffering.

The joy I refer to here can be better defined as the opposite of suffering, or, the cessation of suffering. An example is the kind of feeling one enjoys when one can fall asleep quickly and soundly without drugs, after suffering insomnia for many years, or when one is able to rest after a number of hectic days in a political campaign or a demanding day in the business world. One might find oneself enjoying that relaxation in a mountain-lake region. As one gazes at the high, snowcapped mountains and the huge pine trees, the world and its worries seem a thousand miles away; one feels so small, yet at the same time so great, that one feels alone in the universe.

In Buddhism, there are several ways to classify hu-

man suffering. The most common is a listing of eight categories of suffering:

1. Suffering because of birth.

Although no one remembers the pain experienced upon
leaving the mother's womb, the very fact that a newborn
cries rather than smiles indicates that there is no bliss at
birth.

2. Suffering because of age.

Although aging is a slow process that takes place over
a number of years, the sometimes sudden realization of the
reduction of youthful strength and ability is a painful experience for most people past the age of sixty. Evidence of
this feeling could be found on a visit to a home for the aged,
or simply by speaking to any older person on the subject.

3. Suffering because of sickness.

Very few people can claim immunity to sickness or
injury. I do not have to elaborate on the painful experience
of being sick. This kind of suffering is particularly prevalent
among people who live in places where nutrition and medical care are inadequate.

4. Suffering because of death.

The majority of human beings suffer painfully because of their awareness of the inevitability of death. Such
suffering is particularly severe for those who have a strong
ego, great power, or great wealth, as it is very difficult for
them to contemplate giving up these things.

5. Suffering because of separation from loved ones.

Death is considered by most to constitute permanent
separation. One who has had the experience of losing a loved
one knows how painful that experience can be, and that the
suffering it brings can hardly be remedied. Heartbreak,
worry, the expectation of bad news—all these kinds of suffering are expressed through grief and tears by those whose
loved ones have been kidnapped or imprisoned in concentration camps, who have faced the danger of death, been
sent to war, or been forced into an indefinite period of separation because of political circumstances.

6. Suffering because of an undesirable confrontation with
   another person or thing.

   Some occasions for this kind of suffering might be an
unexpected meeting between two people who hate each other;
a beautiful woman being chased by a man she does not like;
suddenly coming face to face with a robber or maniac; turn-
ing a corner and finding a rabid dog or other animal on the
attack—all these encounters can be sources of great
suffering.

7. Suffering caused by denial of one's desires.

   A child will cry when he or she wants a piece of candy
and the mother says no. Other examples are failure to win
the heart of the one you love, or failure in business. One
can also suffer a great deal if one needs money desperately
and is unable to get it.

8. Suffering because of the burning characteristics of the
   human body and mind.

   In Buddhism, this suffering refers to the five aggregates that form the human experience which is the body
and mind. These five aggregates are form, sensation, perception, conditioned function, and consciousness. Examples
of the burning characteristics of these five aggregates are
anger, anxiety, excessive sexual desire, hatred, jealousy—
all these can be sources of suffering.

   Since the joy I refer to is defined as the cessation of
suffering, it becomes clear from the above description of the
eight categories of suffering that the root of suffering is our
concept of body and mind. If we do not have body and mind,
there is no birth and therefore no suffering because of birth.
Without body and mind, aging, sickness, death, and the
other four kinds of suffering have no base from which to
operate. Therefore, the root of all human suffering is the
human concept of, and attachment to, body and mind. As
in the case of the concept of birth and death, and the concept
of karma, the complete cessation of suffering can only be
achieved by the realization of our basic nature. This means
the realization that the body and mind, which appear to our

sensory organs to exist, are changing from moment to moment, and are impermanent and unreal. It is as if one saw oneself in a dream, or were an actor playing a part. All comes to be defined as emptiness.

Therefore, the realization of basic nature means complete cessation of suffering, which means ultimate joy. The conclusion of this theoretical analysis, which I have earlier referred to as Path 3,* is that our own basic nature is the source of true joy. May I repeat that: *Our own basic nature is the source of joy.*

Now this sounds great, but it is just like saying the clear autumn sky is the source of cheer at a time when the sky is heavily overcast and it is raining, if not storming. Buddhism is not just a philosophical study. One who knows everything in theory about swimming but has never practiced in the water will still face the possibility of drowning if he or she falls into deep water. Buddhism places much emphasis on practice. So, to realize basic nature one must practice according to those methods that I have called Path 1 and Path 2.

Path 1 is designed for the person who is able to divorce himself or herself entirely from worldly affairs and to practice vigorously the concentration of the mind on one point. This method is analogous to launching a rocket from crowded Times Square in New York City on a stormy day with thick clouds. Now just imagine how difficult it would be to fire a rocket under such conditions. Many rockets, even when launched successfully, probably would fall back to earth without ever having reached the upper level of clouds. Only the ones that have enough strength to ascend nonstop can penetrate the heavy cloud cover. The instruments in those rockets that do make it will suddenly detect bright sunshine and the endless deep blue sky in all directions. At that time, what the instruments will detect is vast space, quietness, clarity, and emptiness. Crowded and noisy Times Square in New York City, and even the whole earth, will become so small by comparison that they lose their significance entirely.

*See above, p. 66 et seq.

A similar breakthrough in the human mind, accord-ing to Buddhism, is called enlightenment. At the moment of enlightenment, our basic nature reveals vastness, lim-itlessness, and an incomprehensible nature beyond descrip-tion. All the habits, desires, discriminations, and attachments of human beings become insignificant. The concepts of birth and death, karma, and suffering are there-fore inapplicable. One who achieves this status is said to be enlightened. Buddha Shakyamuni was a human being born more than 2,500 years ago in the land known today as Nepal. He achieved enlightenment at the age of thirty-five and thereby set an excellent example for all human beings.

As I said before, Path 1 is designed for one who is able to divorce himself or herself entirely from worldly affairs and to practice vigorously, just like the Buddha who gave up the king's throne that awaited him and went to the moun-tains to take up difficult ascetic practices. Such a path is like attempting to dig out the root of a big tree without first cutting down the branches. It should be understood to be the highest standard that a human being can possibly achieve according to the Buddha's teachings. Path 1, however, is not for everyone. Buddha therefore taught many other methods to enable human beings to realize their basic nature. I in-clude these methods under Path 2.

All the methods in Path 2 can be described as aiming at one principle, that is, harmony with our basic nature. Here we should note that the concept of self is still in ex-istence. It is 'I' who am in harmony with basic nature. In other words, at the stage of cultivation which I have called Path 2, the self and basic nature are still experienced as separate entities. All the methods of Path 2 are therefore aimed at the goal of identifying the self with basic nature. Also bear in mind that basic nature is a term chosen for the convenience of people at the mundane level.

When the principle of harmony with basic nature is clear in our minds, every action and every thought in our daily life can offer us abundant opportunities to develop that harmony. At the mundane level, basic nature can be defined as nonduality, nondiscrimination, and no-self; or even more condensed, as nonattachment. Therefore, in our daily life, those actions and thoughts which can be qualified as nonduality, nondiscrimination, no-self, or nonattachment are those in harmony with basic nature. On the other hand, actions and thoughts that involve duality, discrimination, the concept of self, or attachment of some sort are not in harmony with basic nature.

Now I wish to give you a few examples of how to practice in harmony with basic nature. These techniques have been useful in my personal practice. But, since each person has different karma, you may find another method more effective.

1. Fifteen minutes a day of meditation on vast space.

You look at the open sky on a clear day. Concentrate your effort to see as far out as you can. If a bird, an airplane, a wisp of cloud, or any other object comes into view, ignore it and don't let it distract you. If your eyes become tired, close them, but your mind should continuously "look" at the vast sky without wavering. The key to this practice can be found in the following verse taken from *The Hundred Thousand Songs of Milarepa*, translated by Garma C.C. Chang*:

> Like the sky devoid of edge or center,
> Meditate on vastness and infinity.

That is the teaching Milarepa gave to his female disciple, Sahle Aiu. It clearly emphasizes nonduality, nondiscrimination, and no-self.

2. Fifteen minutes a day of meditation on energy.

First, think of the outer skin that covers your entire body. Skin is matter and is therefore a form of energy. Next, think of your flesh. Flesh is matter and therefore also a form of energy. The bones are also a form of energy. Further, your lungs, heart, stomach—every part of your body from the outside to the inside, and then from the inside to the outside—is a form of energy.

When you first begin this practice, repeat the process

---

*Boulder: Shambala Publications, 1977.

several times. You will reach the conclusion that everything in your body, as well as your body as a whole, is energy and nothing else.

Then realize that whatever you are sitting on is matter, and thus energy. The air is energy. The warmth of the air is energy. Light is energy. People and animals are energy. The room, the house, the village, the city, the earth, the moon, the sun—everything in boundless space that you can think of is all energy. All is characterized by nonduality and nondiscrimination.

Whenever your mind wavers and you cannot keep expanding your vision of energy while meditating thusly, retreat to a point where your vision of energy is clear.

Since energy is a good analogy for basic nature, this practice can be very effective. It is simple, yet in harmony with the profound level of basic nature.

I presume that you all know how to sit in meditation, so I shall not describe it here. My essay "What We Can Learn From Buddhism" gives a brief description of the sitting positions.* You might like to use it as a reference.

3. Practicing the perfection of giving (dana paramita).

Giving means to help or benefit others. Twenty-five years ago, when I first came to this country, I had the distinct impression that the people of this great nation have, in general, a warm generosity and willingness to help other people. I must admit, however, that this good impression has been gradually fading in recent years. I sincerely hope that this trend will be reversed. It is entirely up to each of us. Don't forget that our social environment is the effect of our common karma.

According to Buddhism, there are three kinds of giving:

a) To help or benefit others by giving them material objects.

Food, clothing, shelter, vehicles, money, and many other items of a material nature are included in this category.

*See below, p. 93 et seq. Also discussed in "A Glimpse of Buddhism." See above, p. 26 et seq.

b) To help or benefit others by giving them right knowledge and correct view.

In Buddhism this refers especially to Dharma, i.e., the Buddha's teaching, because according to Buddhism, Dharma is the most important knowledge that can help people to rid themselves of suffering. Broadly speaking, the teaching of the knowledge and skill to enable people to be productive members of society is also classified as giving under this category.

c) To help or benefit others by protecting them from various kinds of danger, and by alleviating their fears.

This is called the giving of fearlessness. People who contribute to keeping a place, say, Central Park in New York City, secure and peaceful are performing the act of giving as defined in this category. To save people from a ship in distress or from places hit by earthquakes, hurricanes, tidal waves, or other disasters are also good examples of this kind of giving. A doctor or nurse who comforts a patient who has great fear is also performing meritorious giving.

All of the above is giving, but it may not be the perfection of giving. You may remember that when we talked about karma, I said at one point that one who does good deeds with selfish motives receives limited merit, while one who does the same good deeds with no specific purpose or desire receives infinitely greater merit. Let me now describe the perfection of giving, which is one of the six paramitas, or perfections, taught by Buddha.

Perfection of giving means giving without duality, without discrimination, and without concept of self. To put it another way, perfection of giving is giving without any idea as to who is the recipient, what is being given, or who the donor is.

Giving conditionally, or with strings attached, is not the perfection of giving.

Giving with the expectation of reward is not the perfection of giving.

Giving with discrimination regarding the recipient,

thinking, "I only donate to the church but not to the school," is not the perfection of giving.

Giving for selfish reasons is not the perfection of giving.

The perfection of giving demands a mind of equality, nonduality, nondiscrimination, and no-self. Such giving is in harmony with basic nature.

For those who have not achieved the ability to be in harmony with their basic nature, intensive prayer to a tangible supramundane authority may sometimes be helpful. In Christianity, the Holy Mother Mary and Jesus Christ; in Buddhism, Buddha Amitabha and Bodhisattva Kuan-yin; the gods of other religions, etc.; all serve effective purposes when one is seriously ill, in danger, desperate, approaching death, and so forth. Prayer, particularly for those who have had faith in one or more of these gods during their lives, can help to restore one's concentration. The unwavering tranquillity of mind is itself a process in harmony with basic nature—the source of joy.

I thank you for your patience in listening so intently during these four sessions. You have probably noted that the key expression in these lectures has been 'basic nature.' It may be helpful to offer you, as a conclusion, the following quotation from chapter nine of *The Holy Teaching of Vimalakirti*, entitled "The Dharma-Door of Nonduality," as translated by Prof. Robert A.F. Thurman.*

> Then, the Licchavi Vimalakirti asked those bodhisattvas, "Good sirs, please explain how the bodhisattvas enter the Dharma-door of nonduality!"

Thereupon, thirty-one bodhisattvas expressed their views on nonduality. I quote three of these expressions as examples:

> The bodhisattva Srigandha declared, "'I' and 'mine' are two. If there is no presumption of a self, there will be no possessiveness. Thus, the absence of presumption is the entrance into nonduality."...

*University Park and London: Pennsylvania State Press, 1976, p. 73 et seq.

The bodhisattva Tisya declared, "'Good' and 'evil' are two. Seeking neither good nor evil, the understanding of the nonduality of the significant and the meaningless is the entrance into nonduality.". . .

The bodhisattva Suddhadhimukti declared, "To say, 'This is happiness,' and 'That is misery' is dualism. One who is free of all calculations, through the extreme purity of gnosis—his mind is aloof, like empty space; and thus he enters into nonduality."

And near the end we read:

When the bodhisattvas had given their explanations, they all addressed the crown prince Manjusri: "Manjusri, what is the bodhisattva's entrance into nonduality?"

Manjusri replied, "Good sirs, you have all spoken well. Nevertheless, all your explanations are themselves dualistic. To know no one teaching, to express nothing, to say nothing, to explain nothing, to announce nothing, to indicate nothing, and to designate nothing— that is the entrance into nonduality."

Then the crown prince Manjusri said to the Licchavi Vimalakirti, "We have all given our own teachings, noble sir. Now, may you elucidate the teaching of the entrance into the principle of nonduality!"

Thereupon, the Licchavi Vimalakirti kept his silence, saying nothing at all.

The crown prince Manjusri applauded the Licchavi Vimalakirti: "Excellent! Excellent, noble sir! This is indeed the entrance into the nonduality of the bodhisattvas. Here there is no use for syllables, sounds, and ideas."

Dear friends, why have I used so many words?
[At this point, Dr. Shen suddenly raised his voice.*]
NOW ANSWER MY QUESTION, QUICK! QUICK!
[The audience kept silent.]
Excellent! Excellent! We have so many Vimalakirtis

*Ed. note: The lines in brackets were added after Dr. Shen delivered this lecture.

here.

[The audience burst into laughter.]

Now you have experienced it. The very moment that you laughed was the moment that you were in harmony with your basic nature. Perhaps you would all like to go home now and practice harmony with basic nature.

I thank you very much.

WHAT WE CAN LEARN FROM BUDDHISM

Delivered at Cathedral of the Pines
West Rindge, New Hampshire
August 29, 1971

Dear friends:

What can we learn from Buddhism? The answer to this question could be nothing or many things; both answers, according to Buddhism, are correct.

It is easy to understand that there are many things one can learn from Buddhism. It is difficult, however, to comprehend that there is nothing one can learn. The very reason you came here today is to find out for yourselves what you can learn from Buddhism. How, then, can the answer be nothing?

If the answer "nothing can be learned" is correct, then the answer "many things can be learned" must be wrong, or vice versa. How can both answers be right? If both answers are correct, would it not be the same as saying that nothing is not different from many things, or that none is identical with many, or that zero is equal to any number? How could this be?

The answer depends on the level on which we communicate with each other. In Buddhism we say that there are three general levels of communication: the enlightened level, the intellectual level, and the common level.

First, let me make it clear that I have not become enlightened. As in the story of the mother frog and her tadpole, I am only the tadpole who has not yet developed legs and who is still waterbound, lacking the actual experience of the warm sunshine or the gentle breeze that the mother frog has experienced on the bank of the pond. So, anything the tadpole says about warm sunshine or a gentle breeze is only repetition or an interpretation of what the mother frog has said. Similarly, since I do not have a direct experience of enlightenment, what I am trying to communicate to you now is only a repetition of what I understand of the enlightened Buddha's teachings.

However, I wish to stress this: A statement such as "none is not different from many" or "nonbeing is not different from being (or beings)" is precisely what an enlightened person would say to us.

In Buddhist literature one encounters many such statements. For example, the *Heart Sutra* says that matter (or form) is not different from emptiness and emptiness is identical with matter. In many other sutras, Buddha teaches that all the phenomena in the universe are identical with emptiness and emptiness is identical with phenomena. Since you and I are also part of the phenomena of the world, you and I are identical with emptiness and emptiness is identical with us both. Can you understand and appreciate this statement? Are you directly experiencing it and not merely intellectually accepting or knowing it?

If your answer is affirmative, I congratulate you and accord you much respect. Since you realize that you are identical with emptiness, you can appreciate that the question of what you can learn from Buddhism is meaningless. You, the subject, are empty. Buddhism, the object, is also empty, since Buddhism is also a part of phenomena. Since both subject and object are empty, the action of learning is superfluous. So, both answers—"nothing can be learned" and "many things can be learned"—are equally meaningless. To say both are either correct or incorrect is irrelevant. They are just like the noises made by a baby or the sound of the wind.

It is important to note that if you truly experience identification with emptiness, no suffering can affect you, for where is your body to receive pain? What is it that undergoes the suffering of death?

For this reason, the Buddha concluded the *Diamond Sutra* with this verse:

> All the world's phenomena and ideas
> Are unreal, like a dream,
> Like magic, and like an image.
>
> All the world's phenomena and ideas
> Are impermanent, like a water bubble,
> Like dew and lightning.
>
> Thus should one observe and realize
> All the world's phenomena and ideas.

However, if you are not yet enlightened, I wish to share with you the following experiences, which may be helpful.

About twenty years ago, when I was in Hong Kong, I asked a monk, Reverend Yueh Chi, how none could equal many and how phenomena could be identical with emptiness. He looked at me and said:

"Once Buddha Shakyamuni was going to speak before a large assembly. He mounted the platform and stood in silence. Then he raised his hand holding a golden-colored lotus, and an inspiring smile appeared on his face. The assembly wondered but did not understand the meaning of the Buddha's action. Then one of the Buddha's great disciples, Mahakashyapa, responded with a smile. The Buddha thereupon announced that the profound Dharma of truth had been transmitted to Mahakashyapa."

After he told this story, Reverend Yueh Chi closed his eyes and was silent. I could not understand his purpose in telling me the story, and I was frustrated by his silence. So I asked myself, "Have I learned something from this story or not?" Just then, I noticed a slight smile at the corners of his mouth, and at the same time I felt a slight smile on my own face. I felt inspired, but I did not understand the significance of my inspiration. Not until many years later did I understand that this was a typical example of communication at the enlightened level.

A few years later someone told me that in order to understand the principle that phenomena are identical with emptiness, one should view phenomena as images in a mirror and emptiness as the mirror itself. Since the images are neither inside nor outside the mirror, and since no one can physically separate image from mirror or mirror from image, the two are identical.

Although I found this a good analogy, I did not think it quite adequate. An image is the reflection of a certain physical object which exists outside the mirror, but we cannot say that outside emptiness there exist objects of which phenomena are the reflections. The explanation, therefore, did not satisfy me.

Then, one day while I was watching television, I realized that the screen of the television set would be a better metaphor for emptiness, and the picture on the screen a metaphor for phenomena. The television screen is "empty" when the electric circuit is off, but when the circuit is on and electronic impulses stimulate the fluorescent particles that form the screen, all kinds of programs appear. Such programs are certainly comparable to phenomena. The essential difference is that a television program is two-dimensional, while phenomena are three-dimensional. A further difference is that we are aware that there is a source from which electronic waves are broadcast for television, whereas we have no idea how phenomena arise. However, despite the shortcomings of this analogy, I felt I had moved a step ahead.

Then I had another opportunity for understanding. This time I was discussing particle energy with a professor of physics. It occurred to me that the universe is filled with an infinite number of motionless, formless, and weightless "particles" of energy which, when stimulated by certain intangible forces, manifest as complicated phenomena. Therefore, the different phenomena we encounter in the universe are simply manifestations of energy. Space, light, heat, fire, electricity, and—as is common knowledge since Einstein— matter are all different manifestations of energy. No matter how complicated the physical object— even a human being—

or how intangible the phenomenon— even the life of a human being—it is the combination of different manifestations of energy stimulated by certain forces.

In short, like the television shows that appear on the screen, phenomena come into existence in the emptiness of the universe. Like the images on the television screen, which are manifestations of fluorescent particles stimulated by electronic impulses, phenomena are manifestations of energy filling the universe, stimulated by certain forces. In Buddhism these forces are analogous to what is called karma. Furthermore, since the television shows are neither inside the screen nor outside the screen, and since no one can physically or logically separate the television shows from the screen or vice versa, they are identical. By the same token, phenomena, including the force (karma) which produces the manifestations of energy, are not inside emptiness nor outside emptiness, and since no one can separate phenomena from emptiness nor emptiness from phenomena, they are identical.

I made this observation to my professor friend, but he shook his head and said that this was not what he had learned in science.

Whether or not this idea can be proven scientifically remains to be seen. The essence of this kind of teaching— that matter and ideas; man, God, and Buddha; form and emptiness; one and many; being and nonbeing, etc., are identical and without differentiation—is very challenging and perhaps beyond ordinary human comprehension. This teaching is called 'prajnaparamita' in Buddhism.

Literally, prajnaparamita means arriving at the other shore through the perfection of wisdom. It is the teaching which introduces the profound realization of the identity of phenomena and emptiness. The state of such realization is called 'shunyata' in Sanskrit. The traditional translation of shunyata in English as 'voidness' or 'emptiness' requires clarification because, as you can now see, shunyata is far from nothingness.

Again, shunyata is the state of realization of the identity of phenomena and emptiness. Since 'phenomena' im-

plies 'many,' and 'emptiness' implies 'none,' the core of
shunyata is the doctrine that none is identical with many,
as I have tried to point out above.

Our communication has moved onto the intellectual
level. It did so the moment I introduced the terms karma,
prajnaparamita, and shunyata and attempted to define them.

Ours is a common dilemma. For the past 2,500 years,
numerous monks, scholars, and laymen have submerged
their lives in the vast oceans of Buddhist literature in search
of the truth of Dharma. The challenge is so great and the
inspiration is so dear that, once they have tasted the profound doctrine of the Buddhist teaching, very few intellec-
tuals can divorce themselves from it.

I tell you this as a warning, because Buddha taught
that enlightenment is not a product of intellect. One cannot
achieve liberation by following an intellectual course. In-
tellectuals tend to spend too much of their valuable time in
study, critical analysis, and debate. They usually have little
or no time for practice.

Once Buddha told a story about a man who was
wounded by an arrow. Instead of allowing his relatives to
find a doctor to pull out the arrow, the man insisted on first
finding out who hit him, the color of his skin, where he came
from, what material the arrow was made of, who made the
arrow, and so on. Buddha said the man would die long before
he could find those answers.

One who studies but does not practice is like a person
who can recite the contents of a huge cookbook but never
goes into the kitchen to prepare food. He can never relieve
his hunger. Practice is therefore a prerequisite to enlightenment. In some sects of Buddhism—for instance, Zen—
practices such as meditation are even put ahead of
knowledge.

Further, intellect, whether in the field of religion, phi-
losophy, science, or art, is a function of the human mind.
The human mind is like a computer that operates on the
basis of the information stored within. The mind receives
its information mainly from the sense organs. Unfortunately, our sense organs are so inferior that they perceive

only very limited information, and our picture of the universe is therefore distorted.

In two previous talks, "The Five Eyes" and "A Glimpse of Buddhism," I used an electromagnetic spectrum chart* to illustrate the fact that our physical eyes can see only a very small segment of the universe, and a sound reception chart† to demonstrate the limitations of our unaided ears. Because the information we perceive through these organs is far from complete, the impressions we obtain, the interpretations we formulate, and the conclusions we draw could be very wrong in any given instance.

Furthermore, the unenlightened human mind is basically a linear operator; it is finite and exclusive; it is "either-or"; it is dualistic. On the other hand, the enlightened mind is all-inclusive, completely spontaneous, nondiscriminating, and all-encompassing. The scope of the ordinary human mind is similar to the view one gets peering through a pipe: one is unable to see the whole horizon. Similarly, one cannot reach enlightenment by the intellect alone.

Therefore, what we can learn on the intellectual level is to accept the challenge of the vastness of the Buddhist teaching, but to avoid being buried by it. The voluminousness of Buddhist literature can itself be a burden and becomes a serious obstacle if one clings to it. One must free oneself from all attachments before one can attain enlightenment. Buddha used the raft as an analogy. A raft is used to cross a river. Buddha asked his disciples, "Would you say that a man is wise if, after crossing a river and seeing that there is a long way to walk on land, he puts the raft on his back and carries it rather than getting rid of it?"

Now let us discuss what we can learn on the common level. Communication at this stage is probably most important, because these teachings are useful and down-to-earth, and can be very helpful in enriching one's life regardless of one's denomination or faith.

*See p. 2.
†See p. 19.

Earlier I introduced the Sanskrit word 'karma.' I said that karma is a kind of force which causes or creates the manifestations of energy that form phenomena. According to Buddhism, each individual has his own karma and therefore his own manifested world.

The second doctrine is that karma functions according to the law of causation; that is, no phenomenon arises without a specific cause or causes. Causes produce effects which themselves become causes, and so on. This is the law of nature. Buddhism interprets this law of nature from the viewpoint of morality, affirming that good deeds produce good effects and bad deeds produce bad effects.

The third doctrine is that the world or the circumstances in which you are now living can to some extent be modified by your own determination and effort, because your deeds are the very causes of future effects. That is to say, you are able to modify or influence your future by your own endeavor. A cause of great magnitude will produce a great effect. Similarly, a karma of small magnitude will produce a less significant effect. In Buddhism, the karma which produces present effects need not have been created during this lifetime, and the effect caused by present deeds may not occur in this lifetime, unless the magnitude of the karma is so great that the effect is perforce immediate and significant.

Based on the above doctrines, Buddha emphasizes a teaching which in essence tells us that we should concentrate on creating good causes or karma. Many ways for creating good karma have been taught by Buddha. I wish to introduce to you two important ways which, based on my personal experience, will produce effects that will make your present life happier and fuller. In my opinion, they should be considered as sources of joy. The two ways are to produce joy through dana, and joy through dhyana.

1. Joy through dana.

'Dana' is a Sanskrit word which, broadly defined, means helping others through giving. To help others be free from the lack of needed material, to help others be free from ignorance, and to help others be free from any kind of fear are all called giving (dana).*

To help others to such an extent that one forgets one's own interests is the supreme meaning of giving. Such giving has its foundation in the realization of the identity of all men, the oneness of you and me. It is nondiscriminative, unconditional, and unlimited, and it draws its strength from pure compassion. This is the giving that Buddha taught.

Giving inevitably brings joy which is spontaneous, true, and lasting. I am sure many of you have had personal experiences of joy through giving. It is interesting to note, though, that if one expects rewards while practicing giving, that expectation diminishes the joy. If you wish to attain full joy through giving you should not expect any reward. The law of nature will take care of the effect. The less expectation and desire you have for reward, the greater your reward will be.

Furthermore, the effect of giving cannot be precisely quantified. For example, the good karma created by a traveler in the desert who shares his water bottle with those dying of thirst is infinitely greater than that created by a millionaire who makes a $10,000 donation to a worthy cause. In fact, our world is not much better than a horrible desert in which millions are thirsty. Your kindness, generosity, wisdom, knowledge, patience, participation, and your few pennies, are all the precious water of giving. We all have much to offer. Buddha says in the *Diamond Sutra* that by reading, understanding, and telling others about even one sentence of that sutra, one accomplishes merit of incredible measure.

The above gives you a basic understanding of dana. This is the first way I would suggest for creating the good karma that will bring you joy and a better life.

2. Joy through dhyana.

'Dhyana' is the Sanskrit word for the Buddhist practice which elevates man's pure awareness to various de-

*For further discussion of giving, see "A Glimpse of Buddhism," p. 28 above.

Full Vajra Position

Half Vajra Position

Cross-legged Position

grees. This practice involves special methods of mental concentration, intuitive apprehension, nonattachment, and so forth. The usual translation of dhyana is 'meditation'; however, if you examine the meanings of the two words carefully, you will find that they are not equivalent. Nevertheless, in this talk I will use 'meditation' as a general term meaning to practice dhyana.

In his book *The Practice of Zen,** Professor Garma C. C. Chang gives a good bird's-eye view of various methods of meditation. Generally speaking, there are three approaches to the practice of meditation: approach through breathing, approach through bodily posture, and approach through mind.

In one of my previous talks, "A Glimpse of Buddhism,"† I described a simple meditation method called 'counting the breath,' which is the first of six continuous steps developed by the Chinese T'ien T'ai sect of Buddhism. The technique is highly respected among Buddhists.

Today I wish to introduce the second approach to you: the approach through posture. Although the cross-legged sitting position is generally accepted by all Buddhists, Tibetan Buddhism and Zen Buddhism put special emphasis on its importance. The following is a basic training method used by Tibetan Buddhists.

The underlying theory of this approach is that man possesses the natural ability to elevate his awareness and to unfold his wisdom so as to reach ultimate enlightenment. To adjust one's body in such a way that one's original ability can be self-developed without hindrance is the objective of this approach. There are seven important points to be observed in this method of meditation. (It will be helpful in the discussion of these points to refer to the illustration on p. 92.)

1. Preparatory step.

Bowing three times in a kneeling position, as done in some religious rites, is usually a good preparatory step for

*New York: Harper and Row, 1959.
†See p. 26.

meditation. Religious bowing, consisting of bending down and extending the whole body on the ground, is even better. From a physiological point of view, this serves to press out used air which has settled in different parts of the body and to relax the muscles and nerves. If you are not used to religious bowing and kneeling, the following suggested practices may achieve the same purpose:

a. Exhale through the mouth gently but continuously a few times. Near the end of each exhalation, bow down to press out more air. You may do this either by sitting with legs crossed while pressing the lower abdomen with your hands, or by standing with arms hanging straight down effortlessly. Always keep your back straight.

b. Loosely shake your arms and hands as rapidly as possible. Relax your shoulders and feel a lowering of your body weight.

2. Cross-legged sitting.

The purpose of cross-legged sitting is to achieve physical equilibrium of the body and to reduce the pumping effort of the heart by bringing the toes closer to the heart. You may sit with both legs fully crossed as shown in Picture 1, with one leg on the other as in Picture 2, or with both legs crossed loosely as in Picture 3. Having both legs fully crossed is not necessarily better than having the legs loosely crossed. You should assume the posture most comfortable for you.

The shoulders and knees are the areas most sensitive to chill and drafts. It is advisable that they be kept warm, perhaps covered by a towel over the knees during meditation.

3. Erectness of the spine.

The purpose of erect posture is to release the tension and pressure on your central nervous system. This is a very important point. In order to achieve this posture one should sit

a. with one's bottom about three inches higher than the ground touched by the legs—this is accomplished by sitting on an inclined meditation cushion—and

b. with one's head inclined slightly forward, but with

chin back, to straighten the back—pushing the chest out should be avoided.

4. Arm position.

After sitting properly, relax the shoulders and arms, and then put the two hands lightly in the lap so the arms are curved. It should be noted that palms are upward with one palm over the other (preferably the right palm over the left), fingers together, and thumbs touching each other lightly. The purpose of this posture is to improve the body's circulation, including the blood circulatory system. The touching of the thumbs completes the energy circuit, but if they are pressed together bodily tension will increase.

5. Tongue touching roof of mouth.

One should not do this too forcefully. Just a light touch will help induce saliva during meditation. The swallowing of saliva not only will keep the mouth and lips moist but has been proven scientifically to be good for your health.

6. The eyes and breathing.

Obviously one should not talk or open one's mouth wide during meditation. Except for one teaching that suggests that the mouth should be open to help relaxation, most teachers advise that the mouth be closed and that breathing be done through the nose. It does not matter whether the eyes are open or closed during meditation. For those who fall asleep easily, it is usually helpful to keep the eyes open; but most people have difficulty concentrating when there are visual distractions. It is also permissible to have the eyes half open.

There is a natural tendency for breathing to become slower, deeper, and lighter as practice progresses. This should be of no concern. It has been taught that breathing through the nose eventually becomes very light and that all the pores of the body and the arches of the feet may become sources of oxygen supply.

7. Dealing with mind.

As mentioned before, the purpose of meditation is to elevate pure awareness. Pure awareness means awareness without thought in the ordinary sense of the word. However, when thought arises, you should avoid stopping it, since the decision to stop thought is itself a thought. Any kind of hallucination should be classified as thought, and therefore no attention should be paid to any vision or sound that may arise. Remember that anything you can see, feel, or touch is an object and not the subject. As your eye cannot see itself, the subject cannot see the subject. Therefore, the "true you" for which you are seeking cannot be perceived by your senses or brain.

It is also important to observe certain points after meditation:

1) One should rise slowly and avoid any vigorous physical or mental activities immediately after meditation.

2) One should do certain exercises, such as rubbing the palms and the arches of the feet, and massaging the various parts of the body which feel stiff or tingling. Walking is also recommended as a post-meditation exercise, and if one already has some experience of this practice it can itself become a continuation of the meditation.

The best time for meditation is in the very early morning after one has had a good night's sleep. It is not advisable to practice meditation when one is tired.

Continuous practice of meditation will bring natural equilibrium both physically and mentally. Physical and mental equilibrium, once achieved, will inevitably bring joy. Imagine the joy of a chronic insomniac who finds he can fall asleep quickly and soundly, or the joy of a tense, highly excitable person who finds he no longer suffers remorse after arguments because he has become much more even-tempered.

In closing, I would like to tell you a story.

Once there was a young monk who was very anxious to become enlightened. He studied and practiced restlessly in a number of monasteries for many years. His mind was full of desire to be enlightened, full of the methods he had learned, and full of anxiety. After visiting many monasteries, he was told of a very wise and accomplished old monk, who was highly respected by all who knew him. So, the young monk went and stayed with the old monk, hoping to learn from him the correct and fast way to enlightenment.

He imitated the old monk in every possible respect, including the style of his hair and the ragged gown which barely covered his body, because he thought that all this would help him to enlightenment. However, three years elapsed and nothing happened.

Then, one day the young monk learned that his master was gravely ill and probably would die. The young monk became very upset and thought, "I have spent three years here and he hasn't taught me any way to reach enlightenment. If he dies, how will I find another to teach me?" So, the young monk went to his master with a knife. He pointed the knife at the old monk, who lay seriously ill on his mat. The young monk said to him, "Reverend master, for three years I have served you, hoping that you would tell me the way to enlightenment, but you have not done so. Now you are very ill and this is probably my last chance. You must tell me the way to enlightenment now or I will kill you."

The old monk looked at the young one and sighed, "My dear brother, even if I have something to teach you, where is the room in your mind to receive it?" The young monk was suddenly enlightened, and he made a deep bow to the old master.

Thank you.

REPORT ON THREE WEEKS OF MEDITATION

Delivered at the Temple of Enlightenment
Bronx, N.Y.
October, 1973

Dear friends:

Last year, during my three-week meditation, I felt my schedule of physical exercise, meditation and sutra-reading was not properly balanced, although I practiced Tai Chi Chuan three times a day. This year, I was fortunate to have met Reverend Ming Chih before I went into retreat. He taught me a set of exercises for the quickening of my vital force (chi氣). I combined two periods of these exercises, two periods of Tai Chi Chuan, and a certain amount of outdoor labor with sutra study and six periods of meditation a day. I found that I enjoyed a greater sense of both physical and mental well-being than I had experienced on former occasions. Thus I realize that a suitable balance of stillness and motion, both physical and mental, is a necessary condition for meditation. An intensive program that overemphasizes any one aspect will cause imbalance, and is not a good method of cultivation.

Today, Reverend Lok To asked me to report on my three weeks of meditation. I am not prepared for this and I do not know where to begin. So instead I will read to you some verses from the *Mahaprajnaparamita Sutra* which I studied during my retreat and have just come to mind. They

were spoken by the monk Sudrisha to the gods, and run as
follows:

> Illusory sentient being
> Expounding illusory Dharma
> To an illusory audience—
> Magical sentient being
> Expounding magical Dharma
> To a magical audience—
> Dreamlike sentient being
> Expounding dreamlike Dharma
> To a dreamlike audience.

The key words of the above quotation, of course, are 'illusory,' 'magical,' and 'dreamlike,' which sound very commonplace and are found in many sutras. Yet it occurs to me that if we apply the formula of the above verses to our everyday life, we will find it capable of infinite variations and endless applications. I used it often during my meditation and found it very rewarding. I shall apply it now to what is happening here at this moment and see if you agree.

Now, you are all gathered here in this Temple of Enlightenment, are you not? So, you are

> Illusory sentient beings coming to pay homage
> To an illusory buddha
> At an illusory temple.

This afternoon, you will listen to Reverend Jen Chun expound on the sutra. You will then be

> Illusory sentient beings
> Listening to an illusory master
> Expounding an illusory sutra.

When we have meals together, are you not

> Illusory sentient beings
> Taking an illusory meal
> With an illusory congregation?

After a while, you will leave the temple, and perhaps you will run into a fierce-looking, foul-mouthed person who is very discourteous towards you. You are just about to get mad, but then you think: Am I not

An illusory sentient being
Looking at an illusory face
And hearing an illusory voice?

When you think in this way, your chances of getting involved in a brawl will be considerably reduced.

This formula can be applied in the same manner to every action, every movement, every deed, every event; in short, everything. Whether or not you view them as such, all the things you see, hear, feel, or sense during the day or night are illusory, magical, and dreamlike. Even you yourself are illusory, magical, and dreamlike.

At this point, you may want to ask: "If everything in our daily life is illusory, magical, and dreamlike, then we are living from day to day in a dreamy state, muddle-headed and mixed-up. Isn't that what you are saying?"

Dear friends, you are exactly right! We are indeed leading our everyday life muddle-headed and mixed-up. But only a few will admit this fact to themselves.

Now try to think! If you reflect on your life, beginning with the moment you were conscious of your own existence, through the decades, up to this very moment, do not the changes of world events and the vicissitudes of life appear to you now as illusory, like things having happened in a dream? Some of them may appear to be even more illusory than a dream. Now think again! Of all that happened to you in the past, not only are such sensations as joy, anger, grief, and happiness gone, but even some of your most intimate friends are out of your life forever. Isn't that illusory and dreamlike? Yesterday still seems to be lingering on, yet when you recollect it carefully, you will find that everything that happened is gone in a twinkling, like a dream, like an illusion. This morning is also gone. Even the present moment seems like an illusion. Do you not think you should say to yourself, "I am in a dream?" The future is that much more uncertain, with all hopes and expectations truly intangible.

Not only is your present life thus, but your past lives were also like this. You have lived and died, lived again and died again, again and again and again, all the time leading a dazed, confused existence as in a dream. You have not been able to free yourself from the ocean of samsara, the ever-revolving wheel of the five planes of existence. Sometimes, because of defilements and their resulting karma, you will even suffer the tremendous pain of being reborn in the evil planes of existence.

So, the most important thing now is not to find out whether or not we are really leading a dreamy, illusory existence, but to learn how we may get out of it. Now, in the *Mahaprajnaparamita Sutra* we find the following lines which state that in order to quit this continuing round of life and death, we must

Practice the Dharma diligently
With a mind that is in consonance
With the wisdom of the all-knowing one,
And with the attitude of nonattainment.

This is the guide-post of life taught by Buddha Shakyamuni, a reflection of his great compassion.

We should note that although our existence, including our selves, is as unreal as an illusion, magic, or a dream, we must diligently practice the Dharma. Unless we, as illusory beings, cultivate the illusory, there is no hope for us ever to get out of this illusory state of existence. We would remain indefinitely engaged in the horrible revolving wheel of life and death. Hence, we must practice diligently—for only in diligent practice is there hope. This life will soon be over. The opportunity we have now could be one in a thousand years. Let us not allow it to slip through our fingers easily!

Now, what is the Dharma? Actually, everything in the world is Dharma. So, "to practice the Dharma diligently" is to live a diligent, energetic, tireless, and industrious life. But this is not to say that we can escape the round of life and death by striving for wealth and fame. The important thing is to live life

With a mind that is in consonance
With the wisdom of the all-knowing one,
And with the attitude of nonattainment.

This means that your diligent, energetic, tireless, and industrious existence must, at every moment, be in consonance with the wisdom of an all-knowing one, and that you must let your mind follow the way of nonattainment. Only by so doing can your life be led properly, with hope of quitting this confused cycle of life and death.

'The wisdom of the all-knowing one' is simply the wisdom of a buddha. It is also a general term that denotes the great vows and myriad deeds performed by the buddhas and bodhisattvas for the deliverence of sentient beings and for the adornment of buddha-lands. Thus, 'with a mind that is in consonance with the wisdom of the all-knowing one' means that our state of mind and wisdom must, at every moment, be in accord with the great vows and wisdom of the buddhas and bodhisattvas, and that every thought and deed must be directed towards adorning the buddha-land and delivering sentient beings.

'Nonattainment' means nonadherence to appearances, nonattachment, and lack of discrimination. If you say, "This Dharmamaster is the one to whom I like to make offerings," this is not the attitude of nonattainment. You are choosing your object—choosing not only a Dharmamaster, but THIS Dharmamaster. You discriminate between whom you like and whom you dislike. Your offerings, then, are only to satisfy your own egoistic need for this Dharmamaster. This is true even if the offerings are free of desire for the reward of blessings. This is attainment, not nonattainment. Thus, although in the first part of the above verse, you are told to direct every thought and deed towards adorning the buddha-land and delivering sentient beings, it is immediately pointed out in the next line that you must not attach yourself to these deeds. As it is said in the *Diamond Sutra*,

> I shall deliver all sentient beings,
> Yet I shall not entertain the notion of having
> actually delivered even one single sentient being.

This is nonattainment.

Because of nonattainment, there will be no such objects as ego or personal identity, nor any desire to seek blessings or to avert calamities. Since even the 'I' does not exist, how can there be such things as blessings or calamities, happiness or fear? To practice the Dharma diligently with such boundless freedom is the unsurpassed teaching handed down to us from Buddha Shakyamuni out of his great compassion.

Finally, I will say something that is quite tainted with attainment. After you have heard my report, does it help you in any way to clear up your mind, or does it make you more confused than ever?

Thank you.

REALITY

Delivered at The Chinese Cultural Association
New York, New York
December 8, 1979
Translated into English by Fayen Koo

Dear friends:

When I went by Times Square today, I saw the usual
bustling crowd along the street. There were men and women,
old and young. All seemed to be in a great hurry. Suddenly
a thought came to my mind: What are they hurrying for? I
thought about it a little longer and realized that all the
myriad people in the world have been spending their lives
hurrying about in this manner ever since ancient times.
Now it might be said that people hurry about to earn a
living, or to survive, but if we look a little deeper, we will
see that there are also those who hurry about for fame,
profit, and power. There are people who plot and scheme;
who murder for money; who kill and commit arson; who
bury themselves in love; who, fascinated by wealth, lose all
self-control.

The world is full of these kinds of people. Their stories
are stranger than fiction. But when you think about it a
little more, you may wonder what is behind all these activities. And you will probably come to the conclusion that all
these activities are the result of clinging to the ego. It's as
if there is a large ego suspended on top of each of their heads.
This ego is the cause of all pursuits of fame, profit, power,
and all contention, infatuation, etc.

There do exist, of course, many altruistic people—
people who are generous, chivalrous, and compassionate,
people who do not tire of teaching or helping others, and
who enjoy lending a hand to the needy. One finds many
thinkers, philosophers, statesmen, and religious leaders inspired by religious doctrines and meditational practices.
These people generally have only a rather faint idea of an
ego. Some of them would consider it to be illusory; others,
nonexistent. Yet, while their egos are considerably smaller
than those of others, they, too, have some kind of concept
suspended high over their heads. These concepts are usually
in the form of a creator God, or gods, or immortals, or nonego.
Some have narrower concepts such as race, nation, religious
sect, political party, etc. While it is possible to suppress one's
ego under the influence of one of these concepts, the concept
itself becomes a transformed ego that continues to hang over
the head, which sometimes can cause even stronger attachment than the usual ego!

The latter group may seem to be diametrically opposite to the former group that aggrandized the ego, but the
two groups are actually the same, since the one is as firmly
attached to the transformed ego as the other is attached to
the ego.

During the last few centuries, a third group of people
seems to have appeared. These people may be classified under the heading of scientist. They are gradually beginning
to question the concept of ego as a result of their study of
cosmic phenomena and the application of mathematical
analysis.

What, after all, is an ego?

According to Albert Einstein, if the speed of a physical
body exceeds that of light, the body will disappear. If our
bodies disappear while traveling at the speed of light, would
our egos still exist? If our egos also disappear, then when
the speed slows down to below that of light, would our egos
return with the reappearance of our bodies? And where would
our egos be during the interval?

When a surgeon is operating on an unconscious and

dying person, will it occur to him to wonder where the person's ego is at the moment between life and death?

When an astronomer is concentrating his undivided attention on the universe, which is innumerable light-years in extent, will it occur to him that his ego is smaller than the smallest mote in the gigantic universe? Or will he feel that it is as large as the universe he is observing?

Even for a half-baked science buff like me, such questions have arisen. When I was giving my speech called "The Five Eyes" a few years back, I used the electromagnetic spectrum chart to demonstrate the different forms of a human being that are observed under different electromagnetic wavelengths.* I explained that my body assumes different appearances, including a formless appearance unobservable to the naked eye, when observed under infrared rays, x-rays, microscope, cosmic rays, etc. My question was this: Does my ego also change with the appearance of my body? If it does, I do not seem to feel the change when, for example, I am being x-rayed. But if it does not change, then where is the ego when my physical body disappears?

I believe that we generally consider our physical body to be connected to our ego. Is this correct? But from what little I know, scientists do not seem to have found an answer to the question: What is ego? They have only raised the question. Yet just by posing the question, some scientists already have a weaker attachment to their ego than do ordinary people.

The foregoing is only a very superficial analysis of the numerous classes and categories of people in the world, and the various views of the ego. What I want to call to your attention is the fact that only a very few people will remain in one class or category all their lives. Most people have mixtures of various concepts and behaviors. Even robbers can at times be charitable, and heroes are more often than not romantically inclined. Politicians find it impossible not

*See p. 7 et seq. above.

to match wits with their opponents, and he who talks most about altruism is usually the first to think of winnings in a casino. That is why in the thousands of years of the history of mankind, there are only a very few truly "egoless" religious leaders or statesmen.

So, in the entire human race, from ancient times up to the present, only a handful seem to have been able to free themselves from the bondage of this ego or transformed ego. Most just bustle about here and there, from life to life, remaining all the time in this bondage. At least eight out of ten people suffer pain far more than enjoy pleasure. But the majority of people nevertheless keep pursuing this scanty pleasure amidst great pain, as if they were quite content to spend their whole lives in bondage.

At this point, I recall an interesting kung fu story written by King Yung.

Several first-rate kung fu masters met on the peak of Mount Hua in China to elect among themselves five contemporary top-notch masters. It was unanimously agreed to designate Huang Yao-shih as the "Unorthodox One of the East," Yang Kuo as the "Crazy One of the West," the Reverend I Teng as the "Monk of the South," and Kuo Chin as the "Chivalrous One of the North," But they had left the central position, which was the highest, unfilled.

Now, among the masters present, there was a man called Chou Po-tung. He was extremely proficient in the martial arts, and even Huang Yao-shih and I Teng were known to keep him at a respectful distance. But Chou Po-tung had the disposition of a child, absolutely naive and totally incapable of treachery. Although he was over ninety years old he was called Naughty Old Boy by everyone. Huang Yao-shih and the others deliberately failed to nominate him for the central position, in order to tease and to irritate him as an entertainment for themselves. First they nominated, playfully, a young girl called Little Dragon Maid. Then they nominated Huang Yao-shih's daughter, Huang Yung.

Upon hearing the nomination of Huang Yung, Chou Po-tung unexpectedly clapped his hands and laughed.

"Wonderful, wonderful!" he said. "You call yourselves the Unorthodox One of the East, the Chivalrous One of the North, etc., etc. These names mean nothing to me. But Huang Yung is indeed an unusual sprite. Every time I see her, I feel bound hand and foot, and do not know what to do with myself. It is a beautiful choice to make her the topmost of the top-notchers." Hearing this, everyone was caught off guard.

Then Huang Yao-shih sighed and said, "O you Naughty Old Boy! Naughty, Naughty Old Boy! I've got to hand it to you. You are truly great! Unorthodox Huang never did care much about fame. Master I Teng had always considered fame to be illusory. But you, and only you, have nothing at all in your mind. You never even thought of the term 'fame.' You are way above all of us. You should be the topmost of the topnotchers. We should be called Unorthodox East, Crazy West, Priestly South, Chivalrous North, and Naughty Center." Hearing these appellations everyone cheered and felt funny at the same time.

Now, ladies and gentlemen, Huang Yao-shih, as described in that story, was an extremely smart and arrogant person. Yet he was willing to pay homage to Naughty Old Boy because he was smart enough to realize that if one says that he cares little about fame or treats fame as an illusion, he first must have a concept of fame. Although he does not care for fame or considers it to be an illusion, the concept of fame still exists in his mind, however vaguely. And with this concept in mind, the causes of suffering such as contention, jealousy, hypocrisy, and treachery will inevitably arise. So, when compared with Naughty Old Boy whose mind was truly emptied of even the concept of fame, the others had to admit that they were no match for him.

Let us discuss this matter a bit further. In this world there are, perhaps, some people whose minds are emptied of all thoughts of fame. But there are very few—if not none at all—whose minds are totally emptied of the thought of an ego. If we consider Naughty Old Boy, whose mind was totally emptied of the thought of fame, as having freed himself from the bondage of fame, then we can consider a person

whose mind is totally emptied of the thought of ego as having freed himself from the even greater bondage of ego.
Imagine, ladies and gentlemen, what it is like to be so freed.

I have to admit that I have not yet freed myself from
this greater bondage of ego. Therefore, I am sorry that I
cannot give you a direct and exact description. I can only
bring up a few of my personal realizations as topics for discussion. What I understand is as follows:

First, what is meant by 'freed from' is not like simply
moving from one room into yet another. One does not free
oneself into another world. Nor does it mean that the world
will disappear as a result of this new-found freedom. The
world still exists. The mountains are still mountains, and
waters, still waters. The moon continues to shine in the sky.
But if someone has been freed from the bondage of ego or
the transformed ego, all the temptations, gains, losses, and
restrictions in this world no longer have any power over
one. Such a person is like a shining mirror, which reflects
all kinds of faces; pretty, ugly, happy, angry, etc., but which
is not affected by those reflections in the least.

Second, if one's mind is like a polished mirror, the
world is totally empty; there is nothing in it. Scientists, by
carefully observing and analysing the universe, have come
to the conclusion that everything is really nothing but energy. If a scientist were to use the same line of analytic
thinking in observing this assembly here today, he would
realize that behind all the different forms and appearances,
there is really nothing but energy—the lamp light, the fur-
nace heat, the sounds we hear, the movements we see, and
the things we touch are all energy. Men are energy, women
are energy; I am energy, you are energy; every single thing
in this world is fundamentally energy. Yet energy is empty,
and intangible. Now, the man whose mind is clear as a
mirror can also see what the scientist sees. But he differs
from the scientist in that he does not need to employ analysis. He KNOWS that everything, including himself, is IN
ITSELF empty. This is the state of mind depicted in the
Heart Sutra, which says, "(By insight he) observes that matter is no different from emptiness, and emptiness is no dif-

ferent from matter. Matter IS emptiness and emptiness IS matter." Since there is no difference between matter and emptiness, how can the concept of ego arise?

Third, when a person has emerged in such a state, not only does the concept of ego have no way of arising, but everything in this world is viewed as absolutely equal and undifferentiated, which in the Buddhist scriptures is called 'equal and nondual.' On this level, you and I are equal and nondual; ego and nonego are equal and nondual. Birth-and-death and nirvana (birthlessness), defilement and enlightenment, emptiness and substantiality, gain and loss, friends and foes, . . . are all equal and nondual. I can keep on enumerating them until you are all gone, and still be mumbling "equal and nondual."

The manifestation of nonduality is called Real Manifestation. This is to say, we have given a name to the state of equality and nonduality and we call it Real Manifestation (or, simply, Reality), which is the true visage of the universe. Actually, even this name of Reality is unnecessary. Reality and unreality are also equal and nondual. Giving it a name is like putting a patch of cloud on the sky; the sun will no longer be as bright.

At this point some people might say: "If you look at everything in this world as equal and nondual, then there will be no right and wrong, and no good and evil. What kind of world will we have? I don't think this kind of doctrine is going to do our country or our people any good."

In Buddhism, the sort of person who conceives of such a question is highly honored. Because his thoughts are focused on the welfare of sentient beings, he is considered to be a bodhisattva of great compassion.

Actually, when we talk about merging with Reality, we are referring to a gradual and rather difficult process. Still, it must be admitted that however much we can merge with Reality, there would be that much less ego in the world, and therefore that much less ignorance, hatred, and greed. We have seen that Chou Po-tung, the Naughty Old Boy, was emptied only of the thought of fame, yet already was no longer at the mercy of Huang Yao-shih's teasing tactic.

If he were a person who took fame seriously, he would probably have drawn his knife on the Unorthodox East and started a fight with him. You can appreciate the far-reaching effects in a person who is empty of the thought of ego.

So the problem now is *how* to begin to merge with Reality. I use the word merge here to indicate that a mere intellectual understanding of Reality—to take ego lightly, or to take it as an illusion—is not enough. One must actually realize it by personally experiencing it. Only then can one attain the state of emptiness wherein there is not even a presupposition of ego or nonego.

We acquire the concept of ego as soon as we are born. The concept becomes more and more deep-rooted as we age. It becomes extremely difficult for us to merge with Reality. For the last few decades, I have spent a lot of time pondering over this question. I find that many human limitations obstruct our merging with Reality. In general, we have very little wisdom.

As we have discussed in the talk "The Five Eyes," our eyes can only see the so-called band of visible light in the entire electromagnetic wave spectrum.* This is a very minute portion of the spectrum. Our eyes are totally inadequate in dealing with the rest of it. Further, what our ears are capable of hearing is smaller in scope than that of an ordinary dog, and far smaller than that of a porpoise. There are many sounds in the universe which we, as humans, cannot hear at all. We are also incapable of knowing speeds faster than the speed of light or electricity, nor any temperature lower than absolute zero.

Furthermore, it is very difficult to change our habits. We often follow them automatically without being conscious of them.

Let me tell you a very simple story. At the beginning of a seven-day meditation session, a Ch'an master said to his three disciples, "Starting from this moment, you will not talk." The first disciple immediately said, "Yes, master, I will not talk." The second disciple said, "Look, the master

*See p. 2.

told us not to talk, and yet you are talking!" The third disciple looked at the Ch'an master and said, "Master, I am the only obedient one. I will not talk anymore." Perhaps the three disciples were a little stupid, but this anecdote does show how difficult it is for us to change our habits.

Because we human beings are fraught with limitations and because it is so difficult for us to change our habits, it is inevitable that our knowledge and views are less than accurate. Yet more often than not, we are very obstinate. Therefore, I feel it is not an easy matter for human beings to uncover Reality. Unless someday we can break loose from our bondage and habits, we will probably be tied down forever by our ego or transformed ego.

A few days ago, a friend asked me a question which was quite practical, unlike these abstruse and far-fetched discussions on Reality. I repeat it here now, in conclusion to today's talk.

My friend said he would like to learn about Buddhism very much. His aims are 1) to live a longer life, and 2) to have greater wisdom. He asked if I could teach him a simple method to achieve his goals.

I told him, "An Indian legend has it that when a person is born, the total number of breaths and heart-beats in his life time are already predetermined. If this legend is true, then wouldn't prolonging the time of each breath be tantamount to prolonging your life?" He became intensely interested when he heard this. I said again, "You must also have had this experience: When you quarrel with someone, or when you are angry, your heart beats faster and your breath becomes shorter. On the other hand, if you breathe deeply and slowly, your mind too, becomes steady and stable. Deep breathing is very conducive to sleep. With a steady and stable mind, and a clear head, your wisdom will grow naturally." He also agreed readily to this. We then talked a while about some simple methods of deep and slow breathing.

Thinking about it now, it occurs to me that such methods can also be beneficially employed to help us along our path to Reality. After all, if we can prolong our lives, and

enhance our wisdom, we may increase our chances to uncover Reality. So I would like to present here a simple method
I have learned of deep inhalation and slow exhalation, for
your reference.

Deep inhalation and slow exhalation is often called
breath regulation. It is a basic training adopted by the yogis
of India, Taoists of China, esoteric Buddhists of Tibet, and
all practitioners of meditation in both the Mahayana and
Hinayana schools of Buddhism. The goal is to make one's
breath deep, slow, fine, and long. These four words each have
their own significance, but they are also interrelated.

'Deep' means that when one inhales through the nose,
one should imagine the breath being drawn all the way
down to one's *tan t'ien* (丹田)—a point four finger's breadth
below the navel. Ordinarily, when one inhales, the breath
only reaches the upper half of the lungs. It is easy to see
that this is not a desirable way to breathe. Very few people
cause the breath even to reach the tips of their lungs.

When beginning the practice of drawing the breath
into the abdomen, we can usually only fill up the lung tips
at first. Gradually, and quite naturally, we will be able to
draw the breath into our tan t'ien. At that point the younger
practitioners will begin to experience a warm sensation in
their abdomen.

To be 'slow' means to avoid drawing in one's breath
forcibly. One should inhale slowly and continuously with
one's nose. If, after training, a person is able to make one
inhalation last for over half a minute, he is doing fine. But
he must not force himself. This slowness is not only limited
to inhalation; it is even more important to exhale slowly,
which is not easy for a novice. Some masters teach exhalation through the mouth with a whistling sound which serves
to retard the outgoing breath. But in most teachings, exhalation is through the nose, not the mouth.

'Fine' is the opposite of 'coarse.' When a person is emo-
tionally upset, in a temper, or panting, his breath becomes
heavy or coarse. Coarse breaths are short. On the other
hand, when a person is in a peaceful mood, sound asleep, or
meditating, his breaths are generally fine and light. Fine-

ness here also means 'unbroken,' which is an important point to note. In meditation, a person's breath can sometimes appear to have ceased altogether. Actually, there is still a very fine breath. Such fineness of breath can only be achieved by a long period of training.

'Long' does not only mean the length of time required to complete one inhalation-exhalation. It also refers to the fact that it must be done naturally, not by force. Sometimes a person can deliberately prolong his breath and make a single breath last long time. But the process cannot be repeated, and it results in irregularity of breath which can cause trouble. This kind of long breath must be avoided. A long breath must be cultivated gradually until it is lengthened naturally. Furthermore, a long breath should be maintained not only for two or three times, nor for one or two days. Hereafter, your breath should be slow, fine, deep, and long at *all* times.

I am sorry to have taken up so much of your precious time. I wish all of you prolonged life, enhanced wisdom, and sympathetic compassion generated within you. Through the understanding of ultimate emptiness, may all of you one day gain true realization of Reality and live freely and happily in the company of all sentient beings.

Thank you!

THE ENLIGHTENMENT OF BODHISATTVA KUAN-YIN (AVALOKITESHVARA)

Delivered at the University of Hawaii
Honolulu, Hawaii
February 26, 1982
Co-sponsored by Kuan-yin Temple

Dear friends:

The Bodhisattva Kuan-yin made a great vow to release all sentient beings in the universe from suffering. Numerous miraculous events have been attributed to Kuan-yin all over the world. Because of the intimate relation that he has with us, it is taught that by undertaking his method of cultivating realization, one will obtain swift success.

There is an important passage in the *Shurangama Sutra* in which Bodhisattva Kuan-yin relates how he cultivated realization. In that sutra, twenty-five bodhisattvas, in response to the inquiry of Buddha Shakyamuni, explained their methods of cultivation and spiritual attainment. Afterwards, the Buddha asked Bodhisattva Manjushri to evaluate what had been said. Manjushri pointed out that Kuan-yin's way of cultivating realization through hearing was best suited for the people of this world.

So it is because of these reasons that I have chosen the enlightenment of Bodhisattva Kuan-yin as the topic of today's talk.

Before we discuss Bodhisattva Kuan-yin's method, it

is important that we should have some fundamental understanding about the teachings of the Buddha.

The aim of Buddha's teachings is to release all sentient beings from suffering. The essential point is that all human suffering results from our deluded attachment, which in turn is the product of our object-clinging mind.

Here, 'object' means all objects of consciousness, whether they are in the outside world as perceived by our sense organs and skin, or in the inside world of our thoughts, ideas, knowledge, etc. 'Clinging' means grasping or becoming attached. Therefore the object-clinging mind is the state of mind through which we become attached to objects we encounter, and come to believe that those objects are real. Such attachment is deluded attachment. Because of this deluded attachment, our judgement is confounded. Ignorance, greed, hatred, and suffering result. In short, much of our experience of life is based on assumptions and perceptions which are actually contrary to reality.

To reverse this process, Buddha taught various methods to stop clinging to objects and to contemplate reality with a one-pointed mind. This is the key concept involved in 'dhyana' which is incompletely translated as 'meditation.' The practice of meditation is not just sitting like a block of wood or stone; rather, it is the act of learning to concentrate one's mental energies in a state of absorption. This state is achieved in stages, like an ascent to one peak after another. The goal is not reached until one day you suddenly discover that all your deluded attachments have gone like the wind, leaving not a trace, or even a name to hang onto.

To begin my discussion of Kuan-yin's method of cultivation, I would like to present first my translation of the passage from the *Shurangama Sutra* where he explained his meditation technique to the Buddha:

> First I (concentrated) on the audial consciousness, allowed the sounds that were contacting (the ear) to flow off, and thus audial objects subsided and were lost.
>
> Then, since ear-contact and audial objects produced no effect, the mind remained in a state of clarity,

and the phenomena of motion and stillness no longer occurred.

Meditative absorption gradually deepened; ultimately the distinction between audial consciousness and the objects of audial consciousness was no longer in existence.

Although there was no experience of audial consciousness, meditative absorption continued to deepen.

Then, all awareness and objects of awareness became empty.

The awareness of emptiness expanded without boundary; then emptiness and that which is empty became extinct.

Since all arising and subsiding had ceased, equanimity became manifest.

Suddenly, transcending both the mundane and supramundane, there was an undistracted luminosity in all the ten directions.

As is evident, Kuan-yin's method is based on the process of hearing. Before proceeding with a discussion of the technique, we should first have a clear understanding of the following five terms: 'I,' 'the nature to hear,' 'audial consciousness,' 'hearing,' and 'sound.' I might also state here that these five terms correspond to five degrees of deluded attachment, the coarsest and weakest of which is sound, and the subtlest and strongest of which is our 'I.' The latter is the most difficult one to eradicate. Ordinarily we tend to confuse sound, hearing, audial consciousness, and the nature to hear. But actually there are some important and fundamental differences.

Kuan-yin began his cultivation of realization by recognizing those differences. He practiced meditation by the sea. Every morning, when he woke up and everything was quiet about him, he would hear the sound of the tide coming in from afar, breaking the silence. After a while the sound of the tide receded and he would hear the silence restored. Then, the sound of the tide came again, and again the silence was gone. Kuan-yin studied the coming and going of the sound of the tide and discovered that the two objects—the sound of the tide and the silence—were mutually exclusive, that is, he could not hear them both at once. When the sound of the tide arose, silence ceased. When the sound of the tide ceased, silence arose. Nonetheless, he perceived that they both had something in common: both arose and then ceased; both were impermanent. But not so his innate nature to hear itself; it was always present. The nature to hear enabled him to hear the sound of the incoming tide, but it did not go away when the tide went back out, for then he *heard* the silence. Indeed, if it were otherwise and his nature to hear were to have departed with the tide, then he would not only have not heard the silence, but he would not have heard the next tidal advance either. Thus, although the sound of the tide came and went, the nature to hear itself was not subject to those changes.

It is important to realize that while sound just comes and goes, arises and subsides, we ordinarily "pursue" sound's transient pattern of arising and cessation; that is to say, we seize upon it as being entirely real, and therefore develop deluded attachment. In order to impress you more deeply with this crucial point, let me give an example.

Suppose that someone rings a bell. If he then asks if the bell is ringing, one would answer affirmatively. If he were to ask the same question after the ringing had faded away, one would answer in the negative. Here, language is well in accord with what has actually taken place, for the sound of the bell has, in fact, arisen and subsided. But now, if the bell is made to ring again and the question posed is "Can you hear something?" the situation becomes quite different. While the affirmative answer made while the bell continues to ring would still be correct, the same cannot be said of the negative response given when the ringing has ceased. It is true that one no longer hears the bell, but one can still hear. Even if one is aware of no sound at all, it is precisely by using the sense of hearing that one is aware of silence. So it is clear that while sound just comes and goes, the same is not true of our innate nature to hear. This aspect of hearing, which hears transient sounds, but does not itself change, is what is called the innate nature to hear in Buddhist terminology.

The examples given above serve to illustrate the difference between sound and the nature to hear. Sound arises and ceases without lingering for even a moment. It is impermanent. The nature to hear, on the other hand, is always present; it neither arises nor ceases. Even a deaf man possesses the nature to hear, but due to other impairments he cannot hear sounds.

What then is meant by audial consciousness and how does it differ from hearing?

As we all know, the organ through which we hear sounds is the ear. To be more precise, sound waves from external sources cause the eardrum to vibrate, and this in turn stimulates the audial nerves, which in one's brain give rise to the sensation of hearing. Thus, hearing is the process whereby the nature to hear is stimulated to produce a sensation of sound through the activity of the ear and the brain. Nonetheless, sometimes the sensation of sound may even be produced without the activity of the ear. Over two decades ago, a certain Dr. Vincent, in Montreal, Canada, conducted experiments on the human brain in which he made a small opening in the skull of a woman and touched a particular part of her brain with a pair of very fine electrodes. Suddenly, the woman said that she heard someone singing a familiar song, although there was no one actually singing at the time. When the electrodes were removed, the singing stopped. When the same point was touched again, the singing commenced anew. It is obvious that in this case the sensation of the song was produced through the sole agency of the brain without the use of the ear. This part of the hearing process is called 'audial consciousness.' It is the consciousness of sound itself and can exist with or without the existence of an external sound and the physical ear. Another example of audial consciousness is what one hears in a dream.

The foregoing discussion clarifies, I think, the four

terms used in connection with the process of hearing. To sum them up once more, then, the 'nature to hear' is one's ever-present ability to hear. It neither comes nor goes; neither arises nor subsides. 'Hearing' is the audial process that comes about through the activity of the ear and brain. 'Audial consciousness' is the aspect of hearing that functions solely through the agency of the brain. 'Sound' is the object of hearing, whether it be the actual object perceived through the activity of both the ear and brain, or the audial object perceived by the brain alone. It comes and goes, arises and then subsides. In fact, every sound is actually a series of momentary vibrations, each of which has its arising and cessation. Having comprehended these four concepts in this way, we may proceed to discuss Kuan-yin's way of cultivating realization.

Kuan-yin begins his discourse by saying: "First, I (concentrated) on the audial consciousness" which means "during the first stage of meditation, using my hearing." Here, special attention should be paid to the fact that the Bodhisattva Kuan-yin began his cultivation of realization at the level of an ordinary human being. He had a strong sense of self, of an 'I.' Second, he possessed the innate nature to hear. Third, both his audial consciousness and hearing were unimpaired. Fourth, he heard sounds, such as the sound of the tide mentioned above. We all possess these faculties and the delusions associated with them. This is significant, because in the course of this discusssion we will see how Kuan-yin progressed from his ordinary state and proceeded to eradicate his deluded attachments one by one.

As I mentioned above, Kuan-yin practiced meditation by the sea. By listening to the coming and going of the sound of the tide, he realized that sound is neither permanent nor substantial, but arises and ceases momentarily within the field created by one's innate nature to hear. Nonetheless, one becomes attached to sounds, and as a result, delusion arises. Therefore, by allowing the sounds that contacted the ear to flow off, and thereby being detached from the object sound, Kuan-yin was able to eliminate the delusion that has its origin in sound.

"Allowed the sounds that were contacting the ear to flow off, and thus audial objects subsided and were lost" has two aspects that require study. First, we will examine "allowed the sounds that contacted the ear to flow off." This refers to 'entering,' a Buddhist technical term that denotes contact between a sense organ and its object in the external environment. The contacts of the five physical sense organs (i.e., eye, ear, nose, tongue, and skin) with their respective objects and of the mind with the world of thoughts and ideas are termed the 'six entrances' in Buddhism. The entrance we are considering here is that of the ear, and entering in this case is the arising of the sensation of sound when the vibrations of an external source reach the eardrum.

The meaning of 'flow off' is not grasping, not abiding. In the *Diamond Sutra* it says: ". . . not arousing one's mind by abiding in sound, smell, taste, touch, or mental objects. . ." Here not abiding means that one does not linger on the sensation but rather allows the stream of consciousness to continue to flow freely even after contact is made with the object. Thus, Kuan-yin's phrase "allowed the sounds that contacted the ear to flow off" has exactly the same meaning as does "not arousing one's mind by abiding in sound" in the language of the *Diamond Sutra*.

To be precise, 'allowing to flow' means that one does not cling to every single sound heard by the ear in contact with the external world. One should allow each sound to pass away, like water flowing in a stream. This is easy enough to say, but it is quite a feat to accomplish. Our difficulty lies in the fact that we have an established habit whereby we catch hold of single sounds, string them together to form words and sentences, and then impart meanings to them. From this process, deluded attachments, turbulent emotions, and sufferings arise. We can confirm this by means of a simple experiment:

Let someone produce a sequence of single syllables, for example: KUAN SHIH YIN. Now if you were asked what you heard, you might very well reply, "Kuan-shih-yin." Such a response would indicate that at the time you heard those syllables you had not allowed each of the syllables 'kuan' and 'shih' and 'yin' to flow on after entering; you retained them all, strung them together, and made up the word 'Kuan-shih-yin.' You might also associate everything you have ever heard about Bodhisattva Kuan-shih-yin with these sounds. This exemplifies deluded attachment. It does not matter at all whether 'Kuan-shih-yin' is a good or bad term, deluded attachment is deluded attachment all the same. Therefore, in order to get rid of deluded attachments one must allow any and every single sound to flow off.

At this point one might object to all this with the idea that it is just not possible for us to allow sounds to flow without abiding. it would seem that our brains are constructed in such a way as to make us automatically string monosyllables together. This, however, is not entirely true. If we consider this carefully, we will find that allowing sounds to flow is not at all impossible.

At any one moment our ears are in contact with many external sounds: sounds of passing vehicles, of children calling to one another and crying, of someone next to us breathing, and so forth. Usually, we naturally allow these sounds to flow without abiding. Right now, you are probably allowing many sounds to flow, but not the sounds of the words I am speaking. This is because you are paying attention to them, for you desire to know what my talk is getting at. Thus in this case, my words are the sound objects that you do not let flow. You cling to my words. This permits you to understand what is being said and to form mental responses. On the other hand, if you were to desist from this and just allow each syllable to flow, you would not be able to put together words and sentences. You would not have grasped the term 'Kuan-shih-yin' in the example given before, nor would you have grasped the meaning of that term. The results of practicing the allowing-to-flow method, when extended to all perception, can lead to some very profound realizations.

To proceed with Kuan-yin's account, we may next consider the word 'lost' in the phrase "the audial object subsided and was lost." This refers to the elimination of any consciousness of the object. 'Audial object' means the sound heard, or anything that becomes an object of one's hearing. In Chinese Buddhist texts one often comes across two terms which mean 'capability' and 'object.' Specifically, 'capability' refers to the ability to perform subjective functions, as in the statement "I who am capable of hearing," or "I who am capable of seeing." The 'object' is the object of this capability, the sound that is heard, or the color that is seen. Many phenomena result from this dichotomy, which is the primary form of deluded attachment. Therefore, becoming detached from the object is to become detached from the object of hearing and all other objects that arise in connection with the object of hearing. This may be illustrated with an example:

A person once said to me: "The New York subway is so noisy that whenever I board a train my mind is disturbed by the rumbling sound." An analysis of this sentence reveals the following sequence of events:

1) He boards the subway train, and his ears make contact with sounds.

2) He retains every single sound (i.e., he does not allow the sounds to flow off, but grasps at them) and perceives noise. This is the first object of hearing.

3) Stringing all the sounds together, he determines that the noise is a rumble. This is the second object.

4) He identifies the rumble as the sound being made by the subway train—the third object.

5) Due to past associations and present conceptualization he determines that the rumbling sound of the subway is a disturbance. This is the fourth object.

Now let us reverse the order and remove attachment to the objects one by one:

1) Recognizing the rumble of the subway one refrains from associating it with the past experiences that cause one to regard it as a disturbance. This is detachment from the fourth object.

2) Recognizing a rumble, one refrains from determining whether it is the rumble of a train, plane, or something else. This is detachment from the third object.

3) Perceiving noise, one refrains from judging it to be a rumble, squeak, or other sound. This is detachment from the second object.

4) Immediately after making contact with individual sounds one allows them to flow off—one refrains from retaining the sounds and stringing them together to form the sensation of sound in the audio-consciousness that is grounded in the nature to hear. Thus, one becomes detached from the first object.

When we reach this stage, we have become detached from all the objects. This is what is meant by allowing sounds to flow off and losing the object.

Now you know the entire meaning of the statement "I (concentrated) on the audial consciousness, allowed the sounds that were contacting (the ear) to flow off, and thus audial objects subsided and were lost." This was the method employed by Kuan-yin during the first stage of his cultivation of realization. By not allowing sounds which enter through the ear to abide in the audial consciousness, one becomes detached from the object of hearing at once. Therefore audial objects subside and are lost.

Kuan-yin continued: "Then, since ear-contact and audial objects produced no effect, the mind remained in a state of clarity, and the phenomena of motion and stillness no longer occurred."

These words indicate that through ceaseless training in allowing the sounds to flow off and letting the objects disappear, one gradually attains a state in which the innate nature to hear becomes free from the object of hearing and the contact of the ear with the external world. The nature to hear becomes thoroughly quiet and clear, and the mind is not torpid, but remains lucid. When that occurs, one feels neither the sensation of motion, for sound is the result of motion or vibrations, nor does one feel the sensation of stillness, for stillness is perceived in relation to motion. At this stage, 'samadhi' (a technical Buddhist term for meditative absorption) has been attained, but there are many degrees of samadhi and progress through them is made in stages. The state described here may be called the initial stage of meditative absorption. At this level two of the five deluded attachments have been removed—deluded attachment to sound, and deluded atttachment to hearing. Nonetheless, having removed only these two deluded attachments, worldly suffering may be greatly reduced. If we can attain just this stage, we will enjoy ample happiness and freedom in this world.

Your attention is invited to the fact that at this point Buddha's basic teaching to "stop clinging to objects" is achieved. Now the next step is to "contemplate reality with a one-pointed mind."

Therefore Kuan-yin did not stop at this point. He made greater efforts and pushed on in his practice, deepening his samadhi day by day. Thus he said, "Meditative absorption gradually deepened . . ."

The level of cultivation of realization described above could have already been attained by many of you, but what follows is entirely concerned with advancing the state of meditative absorption and is thus not easy for ordinary people to comprehend. Therefore, I wish to clarify my own position at this point. It may be that some of those who hear this have already experienced deep realizations, but I myself am just like the tadpole whose mother has just returned from the bank of a pond. She tries to make us young waterbound frogs understand the loveliness of the gentle breeze and the warm sunshine, but we can merely repeat what she has already said. We will only truly understand what she means when we get our own legs and go onto the bank ourselves. Only then will we realize the truth of the Bodhisattva Kuan-yin's words.

Bodhisattva Kuan-yin continued: ". . . ultimately the distinction between audial consciousness and the objects of audial consciousness was no longer in existence."

Bodhisattva Kuan-yin, in meditative absorption, continued to investigate the difference between the concept of the 'I' who is hearing and the object of hearing, because at

the stage he had attained thus far, both audial consciousness
and the nature to hear were still present. In this case, the
word 'audial consciousness' is used to mean the 'I' who is
hearing, or the nature to hear. The object is the object of
the audial consciousness. In the final analysis, he realized,
there is no difference between the two. Therefore, both (the
individual engaged in) hearing and its object ceased completely; that is to say, they merged. At this time, because
the concepts of hearing and the nature to hear were no longer
present, his mind was filled with freedom and pure happiness. All sufferings except those of birth and death had been
eradicated.

Nonetheless, Kuan-yin did not stop meditating, but
continued his one-pointed mind contemplation, and he found
that "awareness and the object of awareness became empty.
Then the awareness of emptiness expanded without
boundary."

This is a higher level of meditative absorption wherein
there is nothing but awareness left. But who is it that is
aware? It is the 'I.' Thus, as long as there is awareness, there
remains this 'I.'

Kuan-yin proceeded to investigate further to find the
difference between the 'I' who is aware and the object of
awareness. In the end he found that there was no difference
between the two, because they were both empty, intangibly
empty. Hence he said, "awareness and the object of awareness became empty . . ."

In this state of meditative absorption he no longer felt
the existence of his physical body, and he was liberated from
the pains of birth and death. The sensation of emptiness
was so pervasive that it was felt to reach the uttermost
boundaries of the three realms and into the infinite past
and future. It was everywhere, and it had no temporal or
spatial limits. Therefore, Kuan-yin described the stage he
had reached as being without boundary. Still, this was not
the stage of perfection he sought, so the bodhisattva cultivated his realization further:

"Then emptiness and that which is empty became
extinct."

This level of meditative absorption was, of course,

higher than the previous one, but even at this stage there remained a sensation of emptiness. Who was it that felt the sensation of emptiness when emptiness was attained? Although he had lost the sensation of a physical 'I' at this point, there was still a vague sensation of an 'I' present in his consciousness. In other words, there was still a slight degree of deluded attachment left. This stage could easily be mistaken for the highest degree to which realization could be cultivated, but there was still one most important step left to be taken. Therefore, instead of stopping here, he took a further step and doubled his efforts in order to investigate the difference between the 'I' who was empty and the emptiness that was its object. At last he came to realize not only that there was no difference between the two, but that even the sensation of emptiness was nonexistent. Therefore, Kuan-yin said that emptiness and its object were eliminated.

At this stage everything that was subject to arising and subsiding, everything that might appear and then cease, such as thought, sensation, mental reflection, hearing, awareness, emptiness, and ego, had completely ceased. Not a bit of deluded attachment remained. All the sufferings of existence had ended. Darkness was totally dispelled and nothing was left.

Therefore, Kuan-yin said:

"Since all arising and subsiding had ceased, equanimity became manifest."

This is the picture of the land as the mother frog had expressed it. One must not take "equanimity became manifest" to mean "equanimity then appeared before me." So that we might not form such a mistaken impression, the Sixth Patriarch, Hui Neng, pointed out that "when total nirvana manifests, it does not manifest in the relative sense of the word." (*Platform Sutra*, Chapter on Opportunity.) At this stage there is no longer any concept of an 'I.' Therefore, the word 'manifest' actually denotes a complete all-pervasiveness and is not a relative term involving a comparative concept. Hence, Kuan-yin continued:

"Suddenly, transcending both the mundane and supramundane . . ."

At this stage every obstacle was removed. All the de-

luded attachments, the stages of samadhi realized in meditation, and the sensations of subject and object were
transcended—none of them were obstacles any longer. The
true nature of reality was revealed and all Bodhisattva Kuan-
yin could say was: ". . . there was an undistracted luminosity in all the ten directions."

'Ten directions' refers to the absence of any fixed center, the absence of a central ego. 'Undistracted' means that
nothing is wanting; it is perfect, unbounded. 'Luminosity'
means a brightness that is totally without obstacles. These
words are used to convey in language the condition of one's
basic nature, attained through the cultivation of realization, though language is not at all adequate here. "Undistracted luminosity in all the ten directions" makes it clear
that there is now nothing but original nature: There is no
buddha, no sentient being; there is not even emptiness. This
is the 'basic nature,' 'original nature,' 'primordial element,'
or 'buddha-nature' described in the Buddhist scriptures. All
these terms have the same meaning.

In the *Shurangama Sutra*, the Bodhisattva Kuan-yin
made two further statements explaining the function that
arises from our basic nature. This function is the universal
delivery of all sentient beings from suffering through the
great compassion and loving kindness that arise spontaneously from the empty nature of the primordial element.
In this state, defilements are identical with enlightenment
and enlightenment with defilements. Such a state cannot
be the object of mundane speculation, for the attempts of
ordinary individuals to grasp this conceptually can easily
cause further delusion. If we become attached to the notion
of the function, obstacles to the cultivation of realization
may arise. Therefore I have left Kuan-yin's two further
statements unexplained. In any case, if one gains an insight
into the nature of the primordial element, the function will
follow naturally, for they are two aspects of one and the
same thing. Tadpoles like me would do much better to just
concentrate our efforts on the practice of allowing objects
that contact the sense organs to flow off, and thus become

detached from objects. This will at least remove some of the mundane defilements and attachments. I sincerely hope that all of you become free from suffering by practicing Kuan-yin's method.

It is said that to be born as a human being is as rare as the early morning star; to have the opportunity to hear Buddha's teaching is even more rare. I might add that to find the opportunity and time to practice those teachings is the rarest among the rare. I sincerely hope that you are among the rarest of the rare.

Thank you very much.

THE ESSENCE OF BODHISATTVA SAMANTABHADRA'S VOWS

Delivered at the Temple of Enlightenment
Bronx, New York
March 1982
Recorded by John Pan
Translated into English by Fayen Koo

Dear friends:

The topic I would like to bring up for discussion today is "The Ten Great Vows of Bodhisattva Samantabhadra," which constitutes the chapter of the *Avatamsaka Sutra* called "The Vows of Samantabhadra that Lead to the Inconceivable State of Liberation." The *Avatamsaka Sutra* is an important Buddhist text that reveals the state of a buddha such as that achieved by Buddha Shakyamuni at enlightenment. It also shows the path to buddhahood and clearly delineates two basic principles:

1) Not to forsake sentient beings.

Sentient beings are endowed with emotions. They comprise a large variety of types, but by and large the beings most intimate to us are humans. So in following the principle of not forsaking sentient beings, the easiest and yet most important factor is not forsaking our fellow human beings. This principle originates in the expanse of Buddha's compassionate mind, where there's room for everyone. The Buddha never forsakes any person, whether the person be pretty or ugly, good or bad, rich or poor. There is no racial or national discrimination, no sexism or ageism. His compassionate mind embraces all with equal favor. His constant hope is that everyone will obtain happiness, be released from suffering, and will advance towards enlightenment. So, to be in accordance with Buddha's mind, we also must not forsake sentient beings. We must constantly bear in mind the meaning of not forsaking sentient beings.

2) To tread the path of a bodhisattva.

'Bodhisattva' is a Sanskrit word consisting of *bodhi* (enlightenment) and *sattva* (sentient being). The term can have three meanings:

1. A sentient being seeking enlightenment. For instance, you who are here today have all made up your minds to seek wisdom and enlightenment. You are sentient beings seeking enlightenment. Therefore, you can all be called bodhisattvas.

2. An enlightened sentient being. All practitioners of Buddhism who have already become enlightened and who possess great wisdom are bodhisattvas.

3. Using bodhi as a verb, a bodhisattva can also be said to be a person who enlightens other sentient beings. In other words, he is a person who vows to enlighten others after his own enlightenment is fulfilled. Such a person, of course, is a bodhisattva of great deeds.

The path of a bodhisattva is the way to harbor one's thoughts, deal with things, treat people, and cultivate oneself. In other words, it is the way a bodhisattva lives life.

In the *Avatamsaka Sutra*, there is a very interesting story about a young man called Sudhana. Sudhana decided that he wanted to seek buddhahood, but he did not know how to follow the bodhisattva path, how to perform bodhisattva deeds. Because of the good roots he had cultivated in past lives, he had the good fortune to come into the presence of Bodhisattva Manjushri who directed him to study under a large number of knowledgeable teachers. Manjushri said, "Good man, to be near many knowledgeable teachers and to make offerings to them is the first condition for acquiring

omniscience. Therefore, you must not get tired of this path."
Thus he recommended that Sudhana first visit Bhikshu
Gunamegha.

When Sudhana came to Bhikshu Gunamegha's place,
he paid homage to the monk and stated, "I have decided to
seek buddhahood to save all sentient beings. Bud I do not
know how to perform the deeds or cultivate the way of a
bodhisattva." Bhikshu Gunamegha then praised Sudhana
highly because the decision to achieve buddhahood and to
save sentient beings is the fountainhead of all merits. Then
he told Sudhana all he knew about cultivation. In the end,
Bhikshu Gunamegha said, "The extent and merits of a great
bodhisattva are inconceivable. My knowledge is limited and
insignificant. Therefore, you must visit many more truly
knowledgeable teachers."

Thus, Sudhana called on one teacher after another.
Everywhere he went, the teacher would give Sudhana all
of his special and expert knowledge. But, in the end, each
teacher would emphasize the same thing; the extent and
merits of a great bodhisattva are inconceivable, and thus
Sudhana should continue to visit other knowledgeable
teachers. Each teacher would introduce Sudhana to the next.

Sudhana's journey took him to 110 cities. He called
on a total of fifty-three teachers and learned many ways of
cultivating bodhisattvahood. When his good roots had gradually matured, he came into the presence of Bodhisattva
Maitreya. Maitreya led him into the Grand Storied Tower,
wherein Sudhana acquired his first intimate vision of infinitude, the boundlessness and self-nature of the Dharma-
realm of suchness. This further strengthened his vow to
achieve buddhahood. Thereupon, Bodhisattva Maitreya bade
Sudhana to return to Bodhisattva Manjushri.

This time, Sudhana was admonished by Manjushri
not to relax his efforts, not to attach himself to any of his
accomplishments, and not to be content with his little merit
and become proud. He needed to make his vows more extensive and continue the search for buddha-wisdom. He
would have to aspire single-mindedly to meet Bodhisattva
Samantabhadra.

This last chapter of the *Avatamsaka Sutra*, which contains the Vows of Samantabhadra, describes the occasion when Sudhana finally came to see Bodhisattva Samantabhadra. The latter, in answering Sudhana's questions on how to perform the deeds of a bodhisattva and how to tread the path of a bodhisattva, prescribed a whole course of practice for him to follow.

Now, you here today have all made the great decision to acquire the so-called insurpassable perfect enlightenment (anuttara-samyak-sambodhi). You all want to know how to do the deeds of a bodhisattva, how to cultivate the ways of a bodhisattva. The answers given to Sudhana by Bodhisattva Samantabhadra are also answers to the questions in your minds. Therefore, this teaching is just the thing for you.

In order to lead you to a deeper understanding of this chapter of the sutra, I suggest that we all chant together the Vows of Samantabhadra.

[The congregation chants the vows.]

You all chanted very well. I could feel the joy in your hearts while you were chanting. This is very good. As it is said in the sutra, "The Ten Vows of Samantabhadra will produce boundless merits in any person who hears them pronounced. If a person can recite these vows with deep faith, they will accompany him when he is on his death-bed. At that time, all kith and kin, power and wealth, will have forsaken him, but these vows will be his guide, leading him forward. In a twinkling he will be reborn in the Western Pure Land where he will see the Buddha Amitabha and numerous great bodhisattvas."

How clear and firm this statement is!

I always feel that the *Amitabha Sutra*, which we often recite, has elaborated extravagantly on the magnificence of the Pure Land of Ultimate Joy and on the merits of the buddhas in the ten directions, but it has only one sentence to say on how one may be reborn there, i.e., "one cannot be reborn there with little merits, blessings, and good roots." As for cultivation, the only instruction is to "make a vow" and "repeat the name of Buddha Amitabha." To vow to be

reborn in the Pure Land, and to repeat the name of Buddha
Amitabha until one has achieved one-pointedness of mind
are undoubtedly the bases of cultivation. However, for a
modern man leading a complicated life, it is very difficult
to achieve one-pointedness of mind by repeating the Bud-
dha-name. The Ten Great Vows of Samantabhadra thus
serve as a supplementary course of cultivation which will
ensure not only a blissful life lacking suffering, but also
rebirth in the Pure Land of Ultimate Joy. This is a compassionate arrangement of the buddhas/bodhisattvas for
which we should be truly grateful.

I will now list the themes of the Ten Great Vows:

1) To pay homage to all buddhas
2) To sing praises to all tathagatas
3) To make extensive offerings
4) To repent all evil deeds
5) To rejoice in other people's merits
6) To request teachings from the buddhas
7) To implore the buddhas and bodhisattvas to remain
   in the world for a long time
8) To follow the buddhas' footsteps always
9) To always conform to the aspirations of sentient beings
10) To dedicate every merit one has accumulated to all
   sentient beings

Today I can merely touch on the essence of the Ten
Vows. Both ancient and present-day masters have made
many detailed commentaries on these vows, which you
should all read. What little I can do today is to give you an
introduction to that teaching. I hope that through this introduction, you gain a foretaste of the wonderful Dharma-
flavor of the Ten Vows.

The most important theme of the vows, I think, is "not
to forsake sentient beings," which I mentioned at the beginning of this speech. All vows have sentient beings as
their objects. There is a very good simile in the text of the
Ten Great Vows—the tree. A large tree is able to bear abundant fruit, verdant foliage, and a wealth of flowers because
it has a large base of strong roots. If the roots are destroyed,

the tree will wither and die, and will certainly not bear flowers and fruit. The Buddha said, "The flowers and fruit are the buddhas/bodhisattvas; sentient beings are the roots." So no one can become a bodhisattva or buddha without sentient beings, or by forsaking sentient beings. All the great vows have sentient beings as their objects. He who forgets sentient beings, forgets the object of his efforts for buddhahood. He would be like a person trying to build a house in midair. How can he succeed?

Further, we should try to realize the spirit of Samantabhadra's vows. When you have a chance to study the text of these vows you will find that Bodhisattva Samantabhadra places a lot of emphasis on the infinite number of objects, boundless states, and uninterrupted time. So we can understand that the mind that is the source of these vows is also infinite, limitless, boundless, and uninterrupted. I will now tell you what little understanding I have of this state of affairs for your reference and discussion.

1) Infinite number of objects.

My dear friends, to make a vow concerning an infinite number of objects is truly a very important and skillful means of achieving buddhahood. Consider the act of paying homage, for instance. Ordinarily, when we make obeisance to a statue of a buddha, we bow only to that single statue, and thus our merits are also limited to that extent. If, on the other hand, our minds are on the infinite number of buddhas in all the ten directions in space and the three phases of time, then our minds too will be expanded to infinitude and become limitless, boundless, and endless. Further, the merits accumulated by making obeisance will also have these qualities.

Such a notion is very interesting. Let me cite an example: Suppose you are looking at a full moon on a still, clear night in the wilderness. You see a full moon and an expanse of light. At this time another person suddenly comes to your side. He too has come to look at the moon. Would you feel that the moon you are looking at has suddenly been halved, or that the brightness of the moon has been dark-

ened by half? Of course not! Even if there are ten people
looking at the moon at the same time, you would continue
to see a full moon with the same brilliance as before. Not
only you, but all the others would also see the full moon
with the same brilliance. And the same is true whether
there are ten thousand or a million moon-watchers. If the
moon shone on only one person, one person would have the
benefit of its brilliance. But, if it shone on a million people,
then a million people would benefit.

Merits are like the moon. The greater the number of
objects, the greater the merits, even unto infinity. Thus,
when you pay homage to the bodhisattvas and buddhas, you
might only have a statue of a buddha or bodhisattva such
as Avalokiteshvara before you. However, while prostrating,
you should repeat Avalokiteshvara's name, and fix your
mind on the infinite number of Bodhisattva Avalokitesh-
varas in the ten directions and throughout the three phases
of time. Then you should concentrate your mind and recite
the names of all the buddhas in the ten directions and the
three phases of time. In this way, you can properly execute
the vow "to pay homage to all buddhas and bodhisattvas."

Let us take as another example, the "dedication of
merit to all sentient beings." When a child is ill, the mother
prays to the Buddha for her son's recovery. Often she will
say "I dedicate all the merits I have accumulated in the past
to my son," as if her son's blessings would be lessened if she
had dedicated some of her merits to another person. This is
exactly the same as the case of the moon-watcher who is
afraid that the brilliance of the moon will be reduced if there
are more people watching it. The fact is, if the mother had
added the statement "May *all* sick people in the world be
released from suffering and have happiness," she would have
expanded her mind to cover all sentient beings. In so doing,
not only would her son's blessings *not* be reduced, but due
to the expansion of her mind and the universality of her
compassion, her son would probably recover sooner. This
type of merit dedication is in conformity with the true teachings of the Vows of Samantabhadra.

2) Boundless state.

'State' refers to the state of one's mind. I remember that a Dharma master once taught me meditation. He first said to concentrate the mind on a point in the body. When this point is clearly visualized, one then enlarges it until it covers one's entire body, then the entire room, then the entire city, the entire nation, the globe, the solar system, the universe . . . the infinitude. When the infinite stage is reached, the mind is totally cleared of obstacles. When this kind of meditation is used to implement one's vows, the state of mind becomes boundless. This technique may be called 'not fencing oneself in.'

What is fencing oneself in? Consider as an example, the making of offerings. If you say, I will make offerings only to Reverend So-and-so, and not to the other reverends, this is fencing yourself in. All such thoughts are limited in (mental) extent. To believe only in Chinese Buddhism, not in Ceylonese Buddhism; to profess only the Mahayana and to be unwilling to study other schools of Buddhism; and to praise only Buddhism, not the merits of Christianity; all these are fencing oneself in, and are limited in extent. Such people will not be able to understand the essence of Samantabhadra's Great Vows. So, when you are cultivating the Great Vows of Samantabhadra, you must be very careful not to fence yourself in. You should learn to expand your mind to reach the perfect state of boundlessness.

3) Endless and uninterrupted time.

Bodhisattva Samantabhadra made it very clear, and emphasized at every vow, that "the thoughts (of mindfulness on the vows) must succeed one another without interruption." The point is that the true application of the vows consists of noninterruption. An example of interruption is if upon waking in the morning, you give rise to the thought of compassion and determine to cultivate the deeds of a bodhisattva, but by breakfast time you realize that the deeds of a bodhisattva are very difficult to perform and you decide to postpone it for a few years. Receding thusly in your convictions, you cause an interruption to take place. Again, you go to the Temple of Enlightenment to listen to an expounding of the sutra this weekend, but by next weekend you are playing mahjong with your friends again. How can your beneficial thoughts and intentions succeed one another without interruption if you behave in this manner? So it is not easy to be persistent and untiring. Unless you cultivate yourselves to place your own interest second, and put your aspiration of helping people secure happiness first, it will be very difficult for you to achieve uninterrupted, constant awareness of the Ten Great Vows.

My own experience in trying to achieve this end is as follows: First I practiced recitation of the Ten Vows until it was done with great fluency. Then I contemplated how to execute the Ten Vows with body, speech, and mind. Gradually I have come to discover that as one leads one's life, working, eating, drinking, walking, sitting, lying down, getting up, . . . it might be possible to naturally, spontaneously, and effortlessly coordinate all of these activities with the Ten Great Vows. This applies to activities of the body, the speech, or the mind. If such a coordination could occur, one could begin to feel that one is progressing on the path.

Thus far I have been presenting an overall interpretation of the essence of the Ten Great Vows. Each vow could be explained further in great depth. I would like to concentrate the following discussion on three of the vows, namely: 1) to make extensive offerings, 2) to always conform to the aspirations of sentient beings, and 3) to dedicate every merit to all sentient beings. I hope that my interpretation and reflections on these vows will stimulate your own consideration of their significance and applicability.

1) To make extensive offerings.

While making offerings, in addition to having an infinite number of objects, having a mental state that is limitless, and maintaining constant mindfulness without interruption, there is one other very important thing: the offering of Dharma. As the sutra says, "Of all offerings, the offering of Dharma is the highest." Why? "Because all tathagatas honor the Dharma." When we give someone a gift, or when we make offerings to our parents, we always try to give the things they like most. The same principle applies when we make offerings to the buddhas and bodhisattvas. Because buddhas and bodhisattvas like most to relieve sentient beings from sufferings, and because the Dharma causes sentient beings to part from suffering and gain happiness, the offering of Dharma is most honored by buddhas/bodhisattvas, and is therefore most meritorious.

Now, what is an offering of Dharma? The sutra enumerates seven types:

The first is to practice as taught. This means to practice the teachings of the Buddha with your body, speech, and mind. If you can do this, you are making an offering of the Dharma, a true offering to all the buddhas and bodhisattvas.

The next three offerings are: to benefit sentient beings, embrace and accept sentient beings, and to suffer for sentient beings. These three are in accordance with the Buddha's teaching on not forsaking sentient beings. If you can accomplish them, you will certainly be praised and approved by all buddhas. So these, too, are offerings of the Dharma, with infinite merits. In this regard, we should note that to benefit, embrace, and accept sentient beings is probably not unfeasible, but to suffer for another sentient being is very difficult indeed. We tend to think, "If it is his own karmic retribution, he should suffer." It is inconceivable that someone else should suffer for him. This is certainly true when we are functioning at the level of common people. Yet it is not always true to say that absolutely no one will suffer for another. Many people present here are parents. Let me ask you, when your children were suffering in illness, did it ever arise in your mind that you would gladly suffer for them if you could? Have you ever heard of a person who, for the sake of love, would go to prison for his (her) criminal lover? The buddhas look upon sentient being as their own children. If we can extend our willingness to suffer for our children to all sentient beings, we would be in accord with the Buddha-mind. The merit of this kind of Dharma offering is as vast as the ocean or the space above us. It is inconceivable.

Now, the last three offerings: to cultivate good roots diligently, not to forsake the deeds of a bodhisattva, and not to part with the bodhi-mind. These are in accordance with the Buddha's instructions for treading the path of a bodhisattva. If you can perform these offerings, you will also be praised and approved by all buddhas, since these too are Dharma-offerings of boundless merits. It is said in the sutra that if you make offerings with incense, lamps, and purveyances, in quantities as large as a bank of clouds, the ocean, or a mountain, to buddhas as numerous as the sum total of specks of dust in the ten directions and the three phases of time, the resultant merits are less than the merits of entertaining one thought of Dharma-offering. I hope you will all comprehend the significance of this statement. It is far more meritorious to entertain even one thought of benefiting sentient beings than to burn bundle upon bundle of incense in the temple.

2) To always conform to the aspirations of sentient beings.

In the *Avatamsaka Sutra*, it is clearly stated that the basic principle for conforming to the aspirations of sentient beings is the benefitting of all sentient beings equally. So, we should care for and attend to any sentient being and treat him or her as we would treat our parents, or even as we would treat the tathagata, without the slightest difference.

However, here we must keep in mind one important point: to conform to the aspirations of sentient beings does not mean that we do everything the sentient being wishes. The criterion is whether we can be of benefit. Four principles are specifically mentioned in the sutra: "To be a good doctor for those suffering from illness; to point out the right road to those who have lost their way; to bring light to those in the darkness; and to cause the poor to discover hidden treasures." Your attention is called to the fact that these four principles are not only limited to physical commodities but also include spiritual matters. Thus, to be a good doctor for those suffering from illness means that we should cure not only ailments of the body but also those of the mind. Buddhism considers greed, anger, and delusion (or ignorance) as the greatest ailments of mankind. One who cures a person of greed, anger, and delusion is truly conforming to the aspirations of sentient beings. On the other hand, if a person asks you to rob a bank with him, and you comply with his desire, you not only have not cured him of his illnesses of greed, anger, and delusion, but you have actually aggravated them. You have not benefitted him at all. Therefore, you are not properly implementing your great vow to conform to the aspirations of sentient beings.

The Buddha-Dharma is a right path. To be awakened to Buddha-Dharma is to acquire the joy of the Dharma and peace of mind. It is the light, the hidden treasure. He who does not have an opportunity to hear the Dharma may be likened to a person at a crossroad, knowing not which direction to follow; a person in the dark; or a poor man without resources. Therefore, if by conforming to his interests, you could cause him to come into contact with the Dharma, whether by leading him to a knowledgeable person such as a monk, by causing him to listen to the Dharma being expounded, or by introducing him to Buddhist publications, you will be conforming to the aspirations of sentient beings, and your merits will be boundless and immeasurable.

3) To dedicate every merit to all sentient beings.

The *Avatamsaka Sutra*'s chapter on the Ten Great Vows of Bodhisattva Samantabhadra may be said to be the consummation of the Buddhist teachings on the bodhisattva ideal. Universal dedication of merit means to dedicate all merits acquired through the practice of the first nine vows (from paying homage to all buddhas, to conforming to the aspirations of sentient beings) to all sentient beings in all worlds in the ten directions. How can merits be dedicated? I refer you to the words of the sutra: "I vow to cause sentient beings to have constant peace and happiness, to be free from all illness, to fail in any attempt to commit evil, and to succeed quickly in good endeavors. I vow to close on them all doors to the lower planes of existence, and show them the right paths to the human and celestial realms and to nirvana." If you wish to learn how to dedicate your merits, you might bear these words in mind. Thus, when you have done a good deed or acquired merits, and you wish to dedicate the merit to a person or for a certain purpose, be sure to recall the paragraph on universal dedication quoted above. The greater the mental horizon while making the dedication, the greater your merits.

The previous quote is on the vow to relieve sentient beings from suffering and to bring them joy. The paragraph next to that in the sutra refers to the aspect of making Dharma-offerings that involve suffering for sentient beings. The paragraph states: "I am willing to suffer for any and all sentient beings who are suffering from the severe retributions of their previously accumulated evil karma, so that they may be liberated." Such dedication is characteristic of the state of a great bodhisattva such as Ksitigarbha who said, "If I will not descend into the hells, who will?" But such vows that fully express the compassion and will power of a great bodhisattva can hardly be achieved by common people like ourselves. We can only try to cultivate the vows gradually. If you can always bear the other fellow in mind, think of him, wish him happiness, and help him eliminate suffering and acquire happiness, then, as time goes on, your mental horizon (state) will automatically expand. You will view all elders as your parents, all young ones as your children, and the thought will arise in you, "Alas! He has done something bad. This will bring bad retribution. Let the retribution fall on me, so he may be free to tread the right paths that lead to human and celestial existence, and to nirvana." For one making a universal dedication of the merits of the Ten Great Vows, such should be his mental attitude.

The world is like a desert. Sentient beings suffer from parching thirst. Even a drop of water will sustain life. We must not refrain from doing good deeds that are small, nor should we do bad deeds that appear insignificant. Consider

the anticipation entertained by Bodhisattva Samantabhadra when he taught Sudhana the Ten Vows. We should
always bear in mind Buddha's injunction not to forsake sentient beings.

May bodhi grow in everyone.

May the infinite Dharma joy befall everyone.

Thank you.

WHY BUDDHISM?

A series of lectures delivered at
The China Institute in America
New York, New York
May 20, 27, and June 3, 1981

Lecture 1:

FIFTY YEARS IN SEARCH OF AN ANSWER

Dear friends:

I was born in China, in a city called Hangzhou, which is considered one of the most beautiful cities in that country. It is in a very scenic area and has quite a few historical Buddhist landmarks.

Although my family is of Buddhist background, I attended the preliminary and junior high schools operated by Christian missionaries. I had to join Sunday services and participate in the Bible reading class when I entered junior high. I liked the Bible and was quite impressed with the missionaries' work, particularly in the medical field and in their attitude towards helping the poor.

In junior high we also studied biology. The teacher was a good one. During one of his classes, he gave us an impressive and detailed description of the structure and function of the human eye, using a colorful model of the eyeball to illustrate. At the conclusion of this lecture, he said, "Now you can see clearly that the human eye is merely a tool. Its effectiveness can change. When the tool ages, we see less effectively."

Suddenly a question flashed across my mind: If the eye is merely a tool, who is it that is using this tool? Let me repeat the question: Who is it that is using the eye tool?

Many school children conceive of this sort of question. But such inquiry usually stops right there, when a teacher or parent says, "Silly child! It is you! Who else is using your eye?"

Only very few people persistently search for the answer to such a question. An exceptional example of the inquiring mind was Albert Einstein, who deeply questioned some of our most basic assumptions about the universe and about reality. As a result of his nonconformity he became a dropout from school. Yet it was his very quality of persistent inquiry which led to his outstanding accomplishments. His contributions to humanity are well known and do not need my further confirmation.

I was not a dropout from school. I did have a question: "Who is the master who uses the tool of the eye?" Yet I accepted at face value the reply, "It is you! Who else is using it?" But on the other hand, the problem still occupied my mind.

When I first thought to question who is using the eyes as a tool, I made an effort to find some illumination on the subject from the Bible. But, to my disappointment, I could find nothing which I felt was leading me closer to an answer.

One day, probably in my third year of junior high, I brought the question to my teacher, who was also a minister. My teacher calmly said, "Dear child. God made you. It is God's will that you possess eyes. Therefore you are the one who is using them."

"But, teacher, who am I? The body, the heart, the brain, or something else?"

"My child, the mystery of God denies questions. You should not ask. Be a good student. Just do what the Bible teaches."

Our conversation ended there.

And so the question remained with me. Then, when I was completing my first year in senior high, I contracted bronchitis. For recuperation, I was sent to my home town Shao Hsing and stayed with my mother.

At this point I probably began to appreciate my mother's values and outlook for the first time. She was a very devoted Buddhist but had learned very little of the Buddhist scriptures. Her dedication to worship reached such a proportion that sometimes it was incredible. To give you an example, I am told that when I was four years old I had a serious illness. My mother then made a vow that she would bring me to a monastery (I forget the name of it) high on the top of a mountain to make a personal offering if my illness could be cured. It was in a severe winter that I recovered. My mother then determined that we should go to the monastery. It took five days of travel to get to the foot of the mountain. The snow was so heavy that the carriage carriers begged my mother to stop, saying that it was impossible to go up to the monastery. My mother was unyielding: "Even if it rains iron, we have to go."

Whether or not my mother's single-mindedness and devotion influenced me is hard to say. But during this half year of recuperation I did learn a great deal about Buddhist faith from her. My mother was particularly devoted to the Bodhisattva Kuan-yin. She told me many stories about Kuan-yin. Later I came to know that the name Kuan-yin or Kuan-shih-yin is the Chinese equivalent of Avalokiteshvara in Sanskrit. Kuan-yin appears in female form in China and is the symbol of compassion. She is also called the Giver of Fearlessness.

A short stanza which is my mother's favorite is in praise of Kuan-yin. I see quite a few people here who understand Chinese. The others who do not understand Chinese may enjoy looking at calligraphy. Anyway I think it is better to first present the stanza in its original language, and then I will translate:

千處祈求千處應
苦海常作渡人舟

The translation runs:

> For a thousand prayers, a thousand responses.
> You always ferry people across the sea of suffering.

This prayer should give you some idea of the tremendous faith and devotion that was felt for the Buddhist ideal of enlightened compassion personified by Kuan-yin.

About the time I recovered from bronchitis, my own interest in knowing more about Buddhism in general was growing. Then one day, the whole family along with quite a few relatives went to pay respect to the Bodhisattva Kuan-yin in a temple on the top of a hill about two hundred feet high.

Three naughty boys, including myself, didn't want to follow the elders walking up on the main path which was much longer than a trail in the back of the hill. So we decided to take the shortcut. I forget now whether or not it was I who initiated this wonderful idea. About halfway up the hill we somehow lost the trail and had to start climbing a cliff.

We were all teenagers and were already quite fatigued at this point. But there was no retreating now because climbing down was even more difficult than continuing up.

Desperate and feeling somewhat guilty, suddenly it was as if my mother was at my side and was telling me with a tone of urgency, "Call Kuan-yin!" My courage and confidence were immediately bolstered, and I felt as if we were both calling Kuan-yin. I moved ahead.

When the three of us arrived at the top, we found that my mother and the others had not yet arrived. We went on into the temple and I was quite moved to see the impressive statue of Kuan-yin there. This was my first visit to the temple.

It was a custom to consult a type of oracle when visiting this temple. This consisted of shaking a container of bamboo sticks until one of them jumped out. Each stick had a number, which indicated to the attendant to give the devotee a particular piece of paper with a message written on it.

I guess the theory of this practice is that when the

mind and body are totally concentrated on the Bodhisattva
Kuan-yin, a type of force is generated which helps to de-
termine which of the sticks fall out. In any case, the message
I received that day greatly shocked and surprised me, and
I think it profoundly affected the course of life I would follow.
I still remember the exact words of the message, which was
of course written in Chinese:

高危安可涉
平坦自延年
守道當逢泰
風雲不偶然

This translates as:

Why choose the high and risky path?
Your years will just naturally be lengthened (if you
    live) the plain and simple life.
Following the Right Way would lead you to peace and
    prosperity.
Great fame and success don't come accidentally.

During that same summer, I began spending time in
my father's library. I was still looking for the answer to my
question concerning who uses the eyes. I suppose I was also
searching to find out who I was.

My father had a good collection of Chinese books,
among which were included many pieces of Buddhist literature. The first book I took off his shelves was a Buddhist
scripture entitled the *Shurangama Sutra*. 楞嚴經 , pronounced *leng yen*, is its Chinese title. This text had a great
impact on my way of thinking.

The *Shurangama Sutra* presents the teachings of the
Buddha, a human being who lived in Northern India. Although Buddha's time was more than 2,500 years ago, he
was able to analyze human nature using a very logical approach. When I first read the scripture I didn't understand
its logic in depth, nor did the analysis specifically answer
my question. Nevertheless I saw that the Buddha's teaching
might be relevant, and I began to disagree with my teacher's
statement that the mystery of God denies questions. I didn't

think that would be God's will, nor could I find such a statement in the Bible. A statement near the beginning of the
Shurangama Sutra was, however, particularly inspiring for
me. This statement concerned the reason or purpose for
searching for the master of our selves, and it especially helped
me to understand why the question had become so important
to me. Buddha said that it is essential to know who we are,
in order to be able to solve our problems. In other words, if
we are unconscious of what causes us to be, feel, and act the
way that we do, we will have no chance to penetrate the
truth of life.

This statement greatly encouraged me to continue to
investigate the nature of the self and the master who uses
the eye-tool.

At this point, let me ask a question of you. Dear friends,
do you agree that the human eye is merely a tool?

The word 'tool' is defined by dictionaries as an instrument which enables a certain function to be accomplished. A tool is merely a temporal means by which another
end is reached. In this sense, the eye is actually a very
marvelous tool. With our eyes we may see many beautiful
things in the world. A normal person learns eighty percent
or more of his knowledge by using the eye.

Yet, this eye is not permanent. It is subject to aging,
illness, even destruction. The effectiveness of the eye clearly
changes as it becomes older.

The function of a tool can be altered or extended by
adding another tool to it. This is also the case for the eye.
By adding a tool such as a pair of glasses, like the ones I
have, the eye's defect of near-sightedness or far-sightedness
can be corrected. By adding a telescope to the eye, the range
of sight is immensely increased. By adding a microscope to
the eye, we are able to see microbes and molecules which
we cannot perceive solely with the naked eye. So there is
no reason to argue that the eye is not a tool.

By the time I had graduated from college I had convinced myself that it is not only the eye that is a tool, but
the ear as well. Whereas the eye is the tool for seeing, the

ear is the tool for hearing. And not only is the ear a tool, but the nose is a tool, for smelling. Continuing along this line of reasoning, I finally reached the conclusion that not only are the sense organs tools, but also the skin is a tool for touching, the various organs in the body are tools for generating and supplying energy to make the other tools function, and, lastly, the brain is the tool for gathering, storing, and analyzing information and giving instructions to the other tools for functioning. If we dismantle all the parts, then where is the master who is using all of these tools? In short, I was not able to find anything in my body which could not be classified as a tool. Can you?

I wish to emphasize this point: The existence of a tool implies that it is separate from the agent who uses it. The tool, being a physical object, is subject to change, deterioration, or destruction, but this does not necessarily mean that the tool's master has changed, deteriorated, or been destroyed. In the same way, the body-tool is separate from the master of the body-tool. The body can change, be damaged, or die, but this truth does not necessarily apply to the master of the body. The identity and characteristics of the master of the body-tool remain a question.

Scientific and technological developments in recent years have made my question particularly relevant. For example, Mr. A's heart can be removed and transplanted into the body of Mr. B. But this does not change Mr. B into Mr. A. The transplant is only a replacement of a tool, which had formerly been used by Mr. A and is now being used by Mr. B.

In another instance, Mrs. C's brain was partially damaged in an automobile accident. As a result, she lost her memory of the past. But she can still understand and retain information in a conversation. Apparently, her brain's function of memory has lost some of its effectiveness. But that is no different from someone whose tool is damaged and is now using an inferior tool. The master remains the same.

In both cases we recognize that it was only the tool that was replaced or partially damaged. The master has remained intact. So who is it that is using all of these tools which constitute this body? Or more specifically, who is it that is now using the ears to listen to what I am saying?

I must be honest with you. Since I don't seem to possess the quality of an Einstein, fifty years have passed and I am still searching for the answer. Today I have nothing to offer you, but wish to share with you this very question. Perhaps with your help we might find the answer when we next meet.

Thank you.

Lecture 2:

THE SUPERFICIAL I

Dear friends:

In the year of 1937, I graduated from college in Shanghai as an electrical engineer. That same year, Japan invaded China. It also marked the beginning of a very unsettled period in my life.

One year later, I was sent by the Chinese government to Germany to join three Chinese engineers already there. Our mission was to prepare for the building of a telephone manufacturing factory back in China. I was responsible for procuring the necessary equipment and machines, and served as the liason with the German company Siemens and Halske.

I was engaged to my wife, Woo Ju Chu, before I went to Germany, and had a strong desire to get married upon completion of my assignment there. So it was not only due to the fact that my country was fighting an invader and that there was an urgent need for a telephone factory, but it was also because of my personal desire that I worked very hard, hoping that we could have everything ready and shipped out by the end of 1939.

In August of 1939, Germany and Russia signed a non-aggression treaty. I was living in Berlin at that time. Tension in this capital city was mounting obviously. Then, on August 31, 1939, rationing coupons were distributed and anti-aircraft guns were erected on many high-rise buildings. On September 1, Germany invaded Poland!

That day I received a telegram from the Chinese government with the simple instructions to follow my own judgement and make my own decision. I had to consider that although all of the machines and tools had been ordered in Germany, only a few had already been shipped out. It would have been a disaster for our mission if I had left at that time. So I decided to stay. The other three engineers, however, could receive no more training and so they left.

In the afternoon I sent them to the Central Railway Station in Berlin and said farewell. A strong feeling of loneliness and desertion overpowered my whole body as I stood on the platform watching the train pull away. I stayed for a long time before I took the Autobahn back to Siemens Stadt where I was living.

That night I was awakened by a sharp air raid siren. As I had been instructed, I took a blanket and went into the air raid shelter. A horrifying situation faced me when I went into the shelter. All the people were wearing gas masks except myself! I was frozen by the realization that I would be the only one to die if this place were attacked by poisonous gas. I finally managed to sit down in the corner furthest from the entrance. I could feel that many people were staring at me. None spoke.

Some of you might have had the same experience. When one is in a desperate and absolutely hopeless situation, one's mind becomes extremely alert and unusually calm. All that my mother had taught me when I was young came to my mind. I called to Kuan-yin.

I asked myself what would happen if there were a gas attack. Suddenly my old question appeared in my mind. Who is the master who is using all the body-tools, and where is that master? Suppose the gas damages or destroys my brain, my nervous system, my heart and my whole body— these all are my tools. What would happen to the master of these tools? Could the gas destroy that too? Who and where is the master?

Then I recalled what the Buddha said in the *Shurangama Sutra*. I began to consider the possibility that the master for whom I had searched all those years is not the true master, but an illusory one which would be extinct if the body were destroyed by the gas attack. But if so, where is the true master as taught by the Buddha?

With the threat of the gas attack hanging over my head I had a strong feeling of urgency to find the answer. But I could not.

I must apologize if I have moved too fast. I owe you an explanation of what I had learned from the *Shurangama Sutra* and why its message inspired me.

The *Shurangama Sutra* records a lively conversation between the Buddha and his disciple Ananda. As I understand it, the Buddha was asking Ananda to identify the master who was looking at the Buddha, listening to him, and felt attracted to the Buddha's teachings.

Ananda gave seven different responses to the Buddha's question. He was having a hard time pinning down just what part of him was looking at, listening to, and felt attracted to the Buddha's teachings. He proposed that the master is inside of the body, outside of the body, beneath the eye, etc., but seven times his ideas were logically disproved by the Buddha.

Ananda then became quite confused and dejected. The whole point of being a follower of the Buddha was to understand reality and the nature of the self. It seemed now that Ananda had totally failed in his search. So he humbly asked the Buddha for some illumination on this matter.

The key word in their conversation was a term, translated into Chinese as 心, (pronounced *hsin*), which literally means 'heart.' Here, heart does not mean the physical heart in the body. It has a meaning closer to the term in the sentence "He wins her heart." In English this term may sometimes be translated as 'mind.' In this case it may be easiest to understand it as having the connotation of 'master.'

Buddha stated that indeed this confusion about the hsin or master was the fundamental source of our problems. He said that in the same way that sand, no matter how it is cooked, will never turn into rice, sentient beings could not be enlightened to the truth and liberated from their suffering as long as they are ignorant of two basic truths, or two aspects of reality.

Buddha then proceeded to explain the whole question from a totally different perspective than that from which Ananda had approached the problem. What he said indicated to me that there may be another, deeper level of the self which transcends the master for which I had been searching. Buddha's statement was concise, but I find it quite difficult and also very profound. Again, I will first write the passage in Chinese before explaining it in English.

一者無始生死根本，則汝今者
與諸眾生用攀緣心為自性者，

二者無始菩提涅槃元清淨體，
則汝今者識精元明，能生諸緣
，緣所遺者。

Now let me try to translate this statement loosely into plain English, as I understand it. Buddha explained to Ananda that there are two basic truths, as follows:

> The first is that you and all beings believe that the object-clinging mind (which grasps at everything it encounters—form, sound, smell, taste, and sensation—and clings to every idea which arises) is your basic self. This is a misconception, and is the fundamental root of the continuing cycle of birth and death which has been going on since beginningless time.
> The second is that your true basic nature is beginninglessly enlightened, is the state of nirvana, lacks birth and death, and is pure and boundless consciousness. All phenomena, including your body, mind, and all things in the universe, appear in your basic nature. But because your object-clinging mind becomes so attached to these worldly phenomena, your basic nature (clouded by the defilements and karma thus created) is forgotten.

Buddha further stated, "Although sentient beings have forgotten their basic nature, it nevertheless functions continuously, day and night, without being recognized."

As I said before, this message of the Buddha was very concise but also very difficult. Although back in 1939 I remembered the statement of these two fundamental truths by heart, I could only appreciate the first one at that time.

The most important idea discussed in the first truth is the object-clinging mind. Here, the term 'object' refers to any object of consciousness. This includes not only everything perceived by the eye, ear, nose, tongue or skin, but also concepts, ideas, knowledge; in other words, everything detected or thought of by the mind. The object can be anything in the outside world, or in the inside world of oneself. 'Clinging' means grasping, attaching to the object, or becoming totally caught up with the object. Thus, the object-clinging mind is the state of mind which is constantly clinging to one or another object, and which believes these objects to be real.

To understand this further, let us consider the present situation. We are now all in this room. It is my object-clinging mind that functions through my eyes to recognize you, and through my mouth and tongue to give a talk. It is your object-clinging mind which listens through your ears to what I am saying. Our object-clinging minds also function through our skin to detect the room temperature, which is neither too warm nor too cold. It is with our object-clinging minds that we understand that this is a talk having something to do with Buddhism.

Now, what is this so-called object-clinging mind? Would you not say that this object-clinging mind is precisely what you have been calling 'I' or the 'self' since babyhood? As in the examples given above, we would usually say, "I see," "I talk," "I hear," "I detect," and "I understand." But in the *Shurangama Sutra*, Buddha rejected this interpretation, by asserting that the object-clinging mind is not the real I!

Buddha's position is extremely challenging and im-

portant because it completely contradicts our established
beliefs. It is probably a point of view that we have never
considered.

What the Buddha said, putting it in even more sim-
pler form is: The I or self to which we are so firmly and
dearly attached is not our real I. Rather, it is simply the
mind which is continuously clinging to various objects. Such
an object of the mind, whether it is a form, sound, idea, or
something else, changes from moment to moment. So the
object-clinging mind perceiving that object also changes from
moment to moment. Because it changes, it is impermanent,
it is superficial, and it is not real.

This was what I concluded that evening in 1939 while
I was sitting in the far corner of the air raid shelter in Berlin.
I realized that all the events that had occurred on that day—
the invasion, the receipt of the telegram, the hard decision,
the farewell on the platform, the horror in the air raid shelter—all were carried out by my object-clinging mind. This
mind had changed from moment to moment. Moreover, the
object-clinging mind, which uses all the body-tools in contact with the objects, would be extinct if my body were destroyed by the gas attack and all the objects disappeared.
Therefore, could it be possible that the master for whom I
had searched all those years was not the real I but only the
object-clinging mind? Then where is the true I ? Does the
real I also use the same body-tools?

I was totally absorbed in the contemplation of these
questions when I noticed that the people in the room were
moving. The entrance door was open. I heard someone saying that it was not a real attack, only an air raid exercise.
It was as if a heavy stone was removed from my head. It
was also as if my object-clinging mind didn't want me to
discover the secret of its true nature. The urgency of trying
to identify the real I suddenly faded as I quickly followed
the others out of the air raid shelter.

During the next few years my mind was fully occupied
by such activities as returning to China from Germany,
getting married, journeying from Shanghai to Kunming

(which is in the southwestern part of China near Burma), building the telephone factory there, and the birth of our first child. Not only did I lack the opportunity to reflect upon the second truth taught by Buddha in the *Shurangama Sutra*, but even the object-clinging mind which I had recognized in the air raid shelter was nearly forgotten.

Then in 1943, I was sent by the Chinese government to India to purchase certain badly needed instruments and tools. On my way home, I took a twin-engine propeller cargo airplane. World War II was still going on. The plane was not air pressurized and was not able to fly above ten thousand feet. So it had to follow along a valley of the Himalaya Mountains, which are over twenty thousand feet high. That day, the weather was terrible. Not only could we not see anything outside of the window, but we were also horrified by the air pockets. With today's airliners you may not have had such an experience. The so-called air pocket means the airplane could suddenly drop several hundred feet and the passengers, without seat belts in such a cargo plane, could be thrown against the ceiling of the plane. The captain had to order all of us to tie ourselves to the bench. What an awful sight!

Furthermore, in order to avoid crashing into the mountain, the pilot was trying to fly the plane as high as possible. The air became so thin that a fat man next to me was already using the oxygen mask. I was having to take continual deep breaths in order to keep my head clear. We had about twenty passengers in the plane. I dared not look at the faces of the others.

The destination was Kunming, China. It was already more than an hour behind the scheduled arrival time. I knew that my wife would be waiting for me at the airport. I could feel her anxiety and worry since Kunming reportedly was heavily overcast and the airport didn't have an automatic landing facility.

A feeling of horror blanketed my mind when I realized the fact that my wife was a young girl alone in that remote city of China. Her parents and other relatives were all in

Shanghai, which was 5,000 miles away and was occupied by the Japanese. What would happen to her if my airplane crashed?

This deep horrifying worry suddenly cut into my body like a sharp knife. My mind became unusually calm and extremely alert. Something which I had not thought of since I walked out of the air raid shelter in Berlin jumped out of my heart—the object-clinging mind! Suddenly I realized that it was my object-clinging mind which was experiencing the worry and anxiety. It was the object-clinging mind which was aware of the danger to myself in this flight and it was the object-clinging mind which feared death. Previously I had always assumed that it was I who worried and had anxiety, it was I who was aware of danger, and it was I who feared death. But did Buddha not say that this is not the real I?

That experience convinced me that the object-clinging mind is distinguished from the real I. Thereafter I used the term 'superficial I' to refer to the concept of I created by my object-clinging mind. The superficial I changes from moment to moment, is impermanent, and is not real. Therefore, this superficial I appears to be the master who uses all the tools forming my body.

But what is the real I? Do I have a real I? I began to appreciate the second truth taught by Buddha. In conclusion of today's talk may I repeat that message:

> Your true basic nature is beginninglessly enlightened, is the state of nirvana, lacks birth and death, and is pure and boundless consciousness. All phenomena, including your body, mind, and all things in the universe, appear in your basic nature. But because your object-clinging mind becomes so attached to these worldly phenomena, your basic nature (clouded by the defilements and karma thus created) is forgotten.

I began to see the light that the answer to my question might lie in this second truth. But how can I reveal it?

I will try to present my understanding of basic nature in my next talk.

Many thanks for your patience.

Lecture 3:

MIRROR AND WAX, FIRE OF WISDOM

Dear friends:

When the war with Japan was over, my family and I moved back to Shanghai. Then, in the winter of 1947, I had an unusual experience.

Although Shanghai was a big city, only a few of its houses provided central heating. It was not uncommon to burn charcoal for heating.

One day, I was preparing to take a bath. A large bowl containing red hot charcoal was set down to warm the bathroom. I entered the room without noticing anything out of the ordinary. The tub was already filled with hot water and I could see some steam rising out of it.

For some unknown reason, I forgot to lock the bathroom door on this particular occasion. I also should mention that the bathroom had a small side window which was closed.

When I was about ready to step into the bathtub, I instinctively felt that something was wrong. Then I lost consciousness, although apparently I was still able to act. As I later reconstructed the sequence of events, I somehow moved to the window, opened it slightly, moved back to the sink, and stood holding the side of the sink. Fortunately I didn't fall onto the hot charcoal which lay between the window and the tub.

No doubt you have all realized that I had been poisoned by the odorless carbon monoxide and was at the verge of death.

Again, fortune had it that my six-year-old daughter Maria happened to approach the bathroom just at that point. She pushed the door, opened it slightly and looked inside with curiosity. I was later told that Maria said, "Daddy is making a funny face and is slapping his leg."

A cross current of fresh air must have flowed between the door and the window, both of which were now slightly open. It seems that my consciousness was partially regained. I noticed a small human figure, about one foot high, which was approaching me. I had a strange feeling of recognition that this figure was myself. The "small I" didn't come right up to me at once, but advanced and receeded several times in an indecisive manner.

Somehow I was aware of thinking, "You should not let the small I move away. If it disappears again you will be dead." Anxiously I thought to slap the back of my neck in order to stimulate the blood flow. But apparently the hand only took half of the order, for it slapped my leg instead of my neck. I was also trying to call to the Bodhisattva Kuanyin, but it seems that my mouth moved without making any sound. In any case, this explains why Maria said that daddy was making a funny face and slapping his leg.

When recalling this event later, I was ashamed to realize that I only called Kuan-yin for help when I was in great danger. When everything was fine I forgot all about Kuan-yin! How many times could a bodhisattva help a person like that?

Anyway, to return to my experience, I would like to ask you, dear friends, what you make of it. After this event, I searched my mind, but had great difficulty in understanding what the small I was, and who was the I who saw the small I? What was the awareness that warned me of the danger of losing the small I? Could the small I be the superficial I that we talked about last week, and could the awareness of the I who saw the small I be the real I?

This was the first time I directly experienced two I's, although such an awareness was rather vague.

After that incident, I studied Buddhism more diligently. I could spend an hour just thinking about some of the interesting and challenging ideas in the *Shurangama Sutra* and other literature. One such interesting passage is the conversation between the Buddha and King Prasenajit.

This king was a great patron and disciple of the Buddha. At the age of sixty-two he was concerned that he might not live much longer. So he approached the Buddha and stated that he wished to know whether or not the death of a person means total extinction.

Buddha asked the king, "Your body has not yet become extinct. So how can you tell that it will die?"

The king replied, "When a log burns, World Honored One, the wood gradually becomes exhausted, changes to ashes, and finally is extinct. So it is with my body."

"How does your face look as compared with when you were a boy?"

"How can that be compared, World Honored One! The skin on my face was soft and smooth when I was a boy. Now, not only have so many wrinkles appeared on my face and my hair turned so white, but also I have all sorts of symptoms indicating that I am an old man."

"Did your face change occur suddenly?" Buddha asked.

"Oh no, World Honored One, it has changed gradually without my realizing it. I noticed the change perhaps after a ten year period. No! I would say I noticed it year-by-year, or perhaps month-by-month, or even day-by-day. Not even day-by-day—when I think of it carefully, I find that my body has actually been deteriorating from moment to moment. It is through this reasoning that I realize the inevitability of the death of my body."

The Buddha agreed with the king's observation about the changes of the body. But then Buddha went one step further. He reminded the king that although his body was continually deteriorating, his basic nature of awareness had remained the same. In order to illustrate this point the Buddha asked the king, "When did you first see the Ganges River?"

The king replied, "At the age of three the Queen

Mother brought me to the river. That was the first time I saw the Ganges."

"Had your awareness of the river water changed when you saw it again at the age of, say, thirteen?"

"No, World Honored One. Even now, at the age of sixty-two, my perception and awareness of the river water remain the same."

"My king! You have said that your face has wrinkled and your hair has turned white. By observing that your face did not have wrinkles when you were three years old, you realized that you have become old. Has not your nature of awareness aged also?"

"World Honored One, it has not!"

"You are right," said the Buddha. "Your face has wrinkled but your nature of awareness has not. A thing which becomes wrinkled is changing. A thing which does not wrinkle is not changing. A thing which is changing will eventually die. A thing which does not change has never changed. It has neither beginning nor end. How can it die? So why are you talking about a total extinction when the body dies?"

This passage is fairly easy to understand. The king realized that if something can be shown to have the inherent nature to change and deteriorate, as does the body, it would always continue to deteriorate and would finally die. The Buddha added that if something can be shown that does not change, even for a moment, that would mean that it has never changed. If it has never changed, it will never change nor die. Buddha showed that although the body of a being is subject to continous change, deterioration, and death, the being's basic nature of awareness has never changed, and it shall not die even though the body of the being dies.

This teaching made quite clear what happened to me in the bathroom. When my brain was under influence of the carbon monoxide, my object-clinging mind stopped functioning. This is what we normally call a state of unconsciousness. But my nature of awareness remained unchanged.

During this short period of time when the instinctive movement to the window and sink, calling of Kuan-yin, and slapping the leg took place, there was no usual concept of I. Duality between subject and object was transcended. Only when I identified the small I and made an effort to keep it advancing did my object-clinging mind take charge again. Therefore, my nature of awareness remained unchanged during this incident, while my object-clinging mind changed considerably.

Once we recognize that our body is a tool, it seems at first glance that it is the object-clinging mind which is using this tool. But the object-clinging mind continuously changes. So on the deeper level, it is the nature of awareness which is using the body tool. If this set of body tools is damaged or destroyed (which means death), the nature of awareness remains unchanged. It is always in existence, even without the body tool.

Some analogies may help you to appreciate more of what I am trying to convey:

A power plant burns coal to produce heat, which boils water, which produces steam, which turns the turbine. Electricity is then generated. The electricity lights up this room. All the elements in this process change from moment to moment but, from the physical matter of coal to the end product of light, they are all different manifestations of energy. The energy remains unchanged. Energy uses different tools, appears in different forms, but it is always energy. Energy is always in existence. The concept of birth does not apply to it, nor does the concept of death.

Again, do we not see the sun rising in the east, moving across the sky, and setting in the west? But does the sun actually move in this way? No! The illusion of movement is due to the fact that we are looking at the sun from the earth, and the earth is rotating on its axis. The sun has no motion. It neither rises nor sets. Even though we on the earth cannot see it at night, it is always there.

Another analogy which may be even more helpful is again from the *Shurangama Sutra*. During the same gath-

ering in which King Prasenajit was present, the Buddha
was teaching his disciple Ananda to realize the distinction
between the object-clinging mind and the nature of awareness. Buddha held up his hand and asked Ananda, "What
do you see?"

"World Honored One, I see your opened hand."

Then Buddha closed his hand into a fist, and said
"What do you see, Ananda?"

"I see your closed fist, World Honored One."

Buddha proceeded to open and close his fist several
times, saying, "What do you see now?"

"Your hand is constantly moving by opening and
closing."

"Is your awareness of my hand also opening and
closing?"

"No, World Honored One, it is not."

"What moves and what stays still?"

"Your hand which I see is moving, but my awareness
of it does not move. My nature of awareness is always the
same, and is unaffected by the constantly changing objects
which are perceived."

The Buddha then confirmed Ananda's understanding.

The incident in the bathroom in Shanghai made me
even more interested in understanding the basic nature
which Buddha talked about in the *Shurangama Sutra*.
Surely my experience did not reveal my basic nature, but
it made it clear to me that there are other levels of awareness
functioning apart from my usual object-clinging mind. However, I still found that whatever I did and wherever I went,
the superficial I always played the central role. Although I
could appreciate the fact that the unmoving nature of
awareness was always present, the object-clinging mind
would inevitably take over and use the body tools.

Then a major change in my life occurred.

In early 1952, I moved my family to the United States
of America. I began to receive instruction in Tibetan Buddhism from Professor Garma C.C. Chang, who was then in
New York.

In April 1963, Professor Chang took me to Colgate College in the state of New York. This is a scenic mountainous region. The trees had just begun to turn green and new life was about to sprout out of the great earth.

The college had a retreat house attached to its chapel. Professor Chang used this place to give me an intensive course on the practice of meditation. He was very polite and said that he was not a guru. He was giving such instruction to me on behalf of his late guru Kong Ka Rinpoche, a distinguished and well-accomplished Tibetan lama.

Under his strict guidance I entered a seven-day retreat, and practiced intensive meditation from 3 A.M. to 10 A.M. each day.

In the early morning of the seventh day he ordered me to stop sitting and to walk briskly in the wooded area without thinking of anything. It was a chilly morning and the first pale light of dawn was visible in the eastern sky.

After I walked two or three miles, my mind became empty. I wasn't aware of my location nor did I try to find the way back. I must have gotten lost but I didn't care. By the time I finally saw the retreat house again it was already near noon.

I walked into the retreat house. Without looking at anyone nor saying anything, I sat down in half lotus posture in the cell assigned to me.

I don't remember how long I sat. Suddenly I noticed some snow flurries falling outside of the window. I had a strange instinctive feeling that guru Kong Ka Rinpoche was with me, although at that time I didn't know that 'kong-ka' means 'white snow' in Tibetan.

My mind became extremely alert and unusually calm. The *Mahaparinirvana Sutra* text which I had put on the small desk in front of my sitting cushion was shining brightly!

This was the first time that I had the experience of extreme alertness and unusual calm without the prerequisite of great danger or a desperate condition as had been the case on the previous occasions. I should also note that this time the experience was a result of my deliberate practice of meditation and cultivation of enlightenment.

This experience increased my interest and confidence in Buddhism substantially. I was convinced that there is something which is much more profound in Buddha's teaching than I had thought. On the other hand I also realized that it is extremely difficult, if not impossible, to get rid of the object-clinging mind. But it was clear to me that it is precisely the object-clinging mind that has to be worked on and transformed, in order to reach the more profound state where my nature of awareness might shine through.

Over the years, in order to better appreciate the way in which an ordinary person like myself might improve and clarify my state of awareness, I developed an analytical model to explain the functioning of the various levels of mind. The model is based on the analogy of a mirror and wax. As you all know, a mirror is bright and its nature is to reflect an image. But if covered by wax, the mirror loses its clarity and ability to reflect. If you want the mirror to function like a mirror, the wax must be removed. This is simple and clear.

Human beings can be divided into various types in terms of this model of mirror and wax. For example there are some people who have no concern for the problem at all. Completely motivated by ignorance, greed, and hatred, they are in fact adding more wax to the mirror! According to the Buddhist notion of karma, such people are destined to regress into lower existences and will also face bad luck, disturbed mind, or hardship even in this very lifetime.

Others who have no knowledge of the mirror and wax but have some religious values and compassion are in a better position. However, their chances of reducing the wax is slim unless they come to an understanding of the necessity of mental cultivation. Therefore their coating of wax remains thick. Their next rebirth will most likely be among human beings.

Still others understand that the wax prevents the mirror from functioning, but they lack the means to remove the wax. They search for the proper teaching, and do a little here and a little there. But they end up only dancing on the wax, perhaps making a few etchings or beautiful and interesting drawings on the wax, but whether they have actually removed any of the wax is questionable. I may be in this group of people.

In addition, there are those who have realized the importance of removing the wax. But what they do? They remove a piece of the wax here and there, analyze it, study it, write commentaries, and give lectures, teachings, and reports. They are usually well-respected, but in the end they may find that their candle is almost burnt down and the wax still covers the mirror. Dear friends, I feel sorry for this group although I am also one of those who respect them highly. Their intentions are good, but they usually end up with the regret that life is too short and time does not wait.

At this point you may be impatient and would like to say that it's fine to have this model of mirror and wax, but it seems to us that none of the groups you described can remove the wax. Can you tell us something which can?

My friends, this is precisely what I have been trying to find out myself. Over the years I haven't found a conclusive technique that I can give you today. But I did develop some guidelines which probably can help you to remove your wax even though you are conducting your normal life as professionals of whatever capacity and as members of your families and communities.

My guidelines are simple: compassion and meditation.

Being compassionate means to make others comfortable with comfort you would wish to have yourself. It means detaching yourself from the illusions of the superficial I. Compassion can eliminate discrimination and transcend duality so that your nature of awareness comes into harmony with nature itself, and your wax becomes thinner.

The practice of meditation makes the mind alert and calm. Remember that wisdom is the product of a tranquil state of consciousness. Put in another way, the confused, emotional, busy, and disturbed mind cannot produce wisdom. An extremely alert and unusually calm mind, however, just naturally produces great wisdom.

Compassion is like fuel and wisdom is like fire. Fire not only melts the wax, it also evaporates it and *leaves no residue.*

Be patient and consistent. Follow the guidelines of compassion and meditation. One day the heat generated by your compassion fuel and wisdom fire will become so intense that not only will all the wax evaporate but all of a sudden you will realize that the mirror is also made of wax, and it evaporates too. As for what may be left—you are the only one who can discover the answer.

To conclude this talk I would like to share with you a dream that I had when I was seventeen years old.

I dreamed that I was in a huge dome crowded with people. Particularly noticeable were many youths with red ties around their necks. I had never seen such a sight before, even in photos. I was told in the dream that there was a revolution going on in that hall and I should leave immediately.

I rushed out of the dome, passing through three gates. I found myself on the bank of a wide stream. I hid among the tall weeds and saw that three or four people with rifles on their shoulders were searching for me. They didn't see me. After they left, I came out of the weeds. A middle-aged lady called me from the other side of the stream. She was knitting with a ball of wool in a bamboo basket hanging over her arm. When I looked at her, an indescribably comfortable feeling arose in my heart. Her expression was a combination of a smile, kindness, and compassion such that I did not want to move my eyes away.

"Why do you stay there? My side is far better," the lady said softly.

I looked up and down the stream. There was neither bridge nor boat. It was much too wide for me to jump across.

"How can I get across the river?" was my reply. Suddenly I had the feeling that she was actually the Bodhisattva Kuan-yin whom my mother had told me about.

"Look!" She pointed to the stream and I found that there were a number of wooden columns sticking out of the water which could easily be used as stepping stones to cross to the other shore.

While stepping across the columns I noticed that the water was very muddy and that there were many ducks swimming and playing in the water. All of a sudden all the ducks turned into human babies who, just the same, were swimming and playing in the muddy water.

I was astonished but had no time to do anything for the babies. But since that dream I never wish to eat duck.

I kept on walking on the columns in my dream. When I was about to reach the other shore I saw a classmate of mine from junior high called Tsien Jen-in who was half drowned in the water. Using my left hand I pulled him out of the water and we jumped together onto the shore. Somehow he disappeared and I stood in front of the compassionate lady.

The lady said, "Now look. This is where you should go!" Looking in the direction to which she was pointing, I saw an unforgettable view. It was a boundless wheat field, with gentle waves of a pure golden color. It looked magnificent and gorgeous. Far away on the horizon, thousands and thousands of reddish golden rays radiated from the sun. I was not sure in the dream whether the sun was rising or setting.

Dear friends, I hear some of you saying, "Mr. Shen, the sun has no motion. It neither rises nor sets!"

Thank you for your alertness.

Many thanks to you all.

GLOSSARY OF SANSKRIT WORDS

Arranged in alphabetical order according to the phonetic spelling we have adopted in this book. Correct Sanskrit spelling is given in italics following each entry.

anuttara samyak sambodhi (*anuttara samyak sambodhi*) 'Insurpassible, perfect enlightenment.' The unconditional and ultimate realization of full buddhahood.

arhat (*arhat*) 'Worthy one' or 'one who has conquered the enemy (of emotional problems).' The highest level of meditative realization according to early Buddhism; reached by many of the disciples of Buddha Shakyamuni. In the Mahayana form of Buddhism it is said that if the arhat lacks omniscient compassion, then there are still subtle obstructions to knowledge that must be removed in order to achieve buddhahood.

bodhi (*bodhi*) Pure enlightened awareness. The essential quality of consciousness that manifests when the mind is clarified.

bodhisattva (*bodhisattva*) One who is committed to helping all sentient beings become enlightened. Traditionally said to reject the total peace of nirvana even though complete enlightenment had already been reached, and to deliberately remain in samsara to aid others. Refers both to a fully realized bodhisattva such as Avalokiteshvara, Manjushri, or Tara, as well as to students who are practising according to the bodhisattva path.

buddha (*buddha*) 'Awakened one.' Buddha Shakyamuni

became completely enlightened—or awakened to reality—
in the fifth century B.C. in India. Some schools of Buddhism
believe that there have been, are, and will be many other
buddhas, appearing in different forms and in different places.
When capitalized, refers to the buddha of our realm, i.e.,
Buddha Shakyamuni.

dana (*dāna*) 'Giving.' Also can be translated as 'charity,'
'generousity,' etc. In Buddhism, gifts are usually defined as
being of three types: material gifts, gifts of knowledge, and
gifts engendering a fearless state of mind.

danaparamita (*dānapāramitā*) 'Perfection of giving.' Performing the act of giving without any mental attachment
to the gift, the giver (oneself), the receiver, or the act itself,
and with no hope for rewards of any sort.

Dharma (*dharma*) The true law. When capitalized, refers
to the teachings of the Buddha, one of the 'Three Precious
Jewels' in Buddhism. When uncapitalized, refers to any dis-
crete phenomena, or element of existence.

dhyana (*dhyāna*) Incompletely translated as 'meditation.'
Refers to the levels of mental concentration, self-observa-
tion, awareness, and transic absorption achieved through
various techniques of mental training. The original form of
the word *ch'an* in Chinese and *zen* in Japanese.

dhyanaparamita (*dhyānapāramitā*) 'Perfection of meditation.' Meditation that is performed without formulating
such ideas as "I am meditating" or "This is meditation."

duhkha (*duḥkha*) 'Suffering.' The basic and pervasive state
of all who are enmeshed in the cycle of life and death, despite
temporary periods of what we call happiness when we don't
observe the situation closely. The three causes of suffering
are the impermanence of all things, the lack of independence
of all things, and the situations we normally associate with
suffering such as illness, death, etc. Eight types of suffering
are also listed.

karma (*karma*) 'Action.' Cause and effect; the natural law of the universe whereby every action produces its appropriate result. Accordingly, the present situation is the natural result of previous causes, or actions. However, there is also complete freedom in this system, since we control our own destiny through our own actions. Moreover, when a person becomes enlightened, the law of cause and effect loses its significance.

kshantiparamita (*kṣantipāramitā*) 'Perfection of patience.' Patience in Buddhism means the endurance of unsatisfactory situations with wisdom; the state of being prepared to cope with dangerous beings with compassion; the lack of feelings of anger, irritation, and annoyance; and the willingness to meditate and investigate the nature of reality for as long as is necessary. The perfection of patience means the discarding of all attachment to oneself who is patient, the object that is endured, and the act of patience itself.

nirvana (*nirvāṇa*) Full and complete enlightenment as to the true nature of all things. The state of being liberated from all suffering. Synonymous with buddhahood.

paramita (*pāramitā*) Can mean 'perfection,' or 'arrived at the other shore,' implying the transcendence of all materialistic clinging and extreme views. Describes the nature of the enlightened activity of a buddha or bodhisattva, in which there is no attachment to the subject, the object, or the action itself.

prajna (*prajñā*) 'Awareness' or 'wisdom.' The penetrating quality of mind that comprehends the nature of reality.

prajnaparamita (*prajñāpāramitā*) 'Perfection of wisdom.' The profound realization of shunyata (emptiness). Refers also to one of the essential teachings of Buddha, and is the name of an important group of sutras.

samadhi (*samādhi*) Meditative absorption; the state of deep concentration and awareness when the mind is simultaneously quiet and clear, unaffected by external sensory input. There are many degrees of samadhi, and also various types, depending on the nature of the meditation being practiced, and the depth of absorption achieved.

samsara *(saṁsāra)* The cycle of worldly existence. The continuous round of birth, death, rebirth, and so on. According to Buddhism there are three realms of existence: the realm where life is dominated by desire, the realm of form, and the realm where there is no physical form. The latter two correspond to certain meditative states; the former, the realm of desire, is the world as we usually think of it and contains five basic types of life forms: heavenly gods, humans, animals, hungry spirits, and hell-dwellers. One of the primary goals of Buddhism is to avoid being trapped in the cycle of life and death.

Sangha *(saṅgha)* The assembly of disciples of the Buddha; one of the 'Three Precious Jewels' in Buddhism. In most contexts refers to ordained monks and nuns.

shilaparamita *(śīlapāramitā)* The perfection of moral discipline. Implies the development of ethical behavior and manners in the general sense, as well as the adherence to the rules of one's specific discipline and maintenance of the vows one has taken. To attain perfection of discipline, one does not, however, cling to the notion of oneself as being disciplined, to the rule that is being followed, nor to the notion of discipline itself.

shunyata *(śūnyatā)* 'Emptiness.' May also be translated as 'relativity.' According to Buddhism, the basic principle of the universe is that no thing exists independently and permanently; all things are interdependent, and arise, abide, and cease dependent upon other causes and conditions. Thus all things are empty of an inherently real self-nature. Two types of emptiness are taught: all beings are empty of a soul or self, and all phenomena are empty of self-nature. It should be noted that the teaching of emptiness does not mean nihilism, or that nothing exists. It is in order to avoid this misconception that the principle of relativity is given as the traditional explanation of emptiness.

sutra *(sūtra)* A type of scripture containing sermons given by the Buddha; one of the sections of the Buddhist canon containing many texts of this type.

Tathagata (*tathāgata*) The 'Thus Come One'; a title or phrase applied to all buddhas. Signifies the profound and ultimate realization of full enlightenment.

viryaparamita (*viryapāramitā*) The perfection of strenuousness, or diligence, effort. The untiring attitude towards meditation and other practices on the path to enlightenment; the strenuousness one applies to helping other sentient beings without being attached to oneself as strenuous, the deed one is performing strenuously, or the state of being strenuous itself.